RESEARCH, RESOURCES AND THE ENVIRONMENT IN THIRD WORLD DEVELOPMENT

edited by J.G. Nelson and K. Drew Knight

Proceedings of the Resources and Environment Workshop from the Conference on "Research for Third World Development, Ontario Perspectives," co-sponsored by the University of Waterloo and the International Development Research Centre, University of Waterloo, May 14-16, 1985.

Department of Geography Publication Series No. 27, University of Waterloo

RESEARCH, RESOURCES AND THE ENVIRONMENT

IN THIRD WORLD DEVELOPMENT

edited by J.G. Nelson and K. Drew Knight

DEPARTMENT OF GEOGRAPHY
PUBLICATION SERIES

Series Editor — Chris Bryant
Associate Editor — Ellsworth LeDrew
Cover — Gary Brannon
Cartography — Barry Levely
Layout and Design — Gary Brannon
Computer Systems Design — Marco Dumancic
Text Preparation — Susan Friesen

Canadian Cataloguing in Publication Data

Main entry under title:

Research, resources and the environment in third
    world development

(Department of Geography publication; no. 27)
Papers prepared for The Resources and Environment
Workshop of the conference Research for Third World
Development: Ontario Perspectives, held at the
University of Waterloo, May 14-16, 1985, and
sponsored by the University of Waterloo and the
International Development Research Centre.
Includes bibliographies.
ISBN 0-921083-23-8

1. Economic development – Environmental aspects –
Congresses.   2. Developing countries – Economic
policy – Congresses.   3. Natural resources –
Developing countries – Congresses.   4. Research –
Developing countries – Congresses.   I. Nelson,
J. G. (James Gordon), 1932-   .   II. Knight,
Kenneth Drew, 1954-   .   III. University of
Waterloo. Dept. of Geography.   IV. International
Development Research Centre (Canada).   V. Series.

HD75.6.R48   1987   363.7   C87-093939-4

Acknowledgements

We are grateful to many persons who made this project possible. First, is Len Gertler, Faculty Coordinator, who was fundamentally responsible for organising the conference of which the workshop was part. Second, we would like to thank Marie Le Lievre, Conference Administrator, who assisted with many details. We would also like to thank all the IDRC personnel involved and specifically, Raúl Vicencio, Associate Director, Earth Sciences, Cooperative Programs Division, who helped organise our workshop and also prepared a key background paper.

We are thankful for the participation and enthusiasm of the persons who attended the workshops and especially Robert Cecil and Nalni D. Jayal, who prepared major background papers along with Raúl Vicencio. Susan Friesen prepared the manuscript for publication with help from Doug Dudycha, Chris Matulewicz and MaryLynn Reinhart. The computer program was designed by Marko Dumancic. The cartography was prepared in the Environmental Studies Cartographic Centre under the direction of Gary Brannon. As editor of the Geography Publication Series, Chris Bryant encouraged us to publish.

We also acknowledge the kindness of the Canadian Arctic Resources Committee, Canadian International Development Agency, *Environments,* and Environment Council of Alberta in granting permission to publish selected figures in the text.

J.G. Nelson

K. Drew Knight

TABLE OF CONTENTS

CHAPTER 3

CHAPTER 4

PART II

CHAPTER 5

CHAPTER 6

CHAPTER 7

LIST OF FIGURES

36-24-36

CHAPTER 1

CHAPTER 6

CHAPTER 7

CHAPTER 10

CHAPTER 12

LIST OF TABLES

CHAPTER 1

CHAPTER 8

Introduction

K. Drew Knight
and
J.G. Nelson
Faculty of Environmental Studies
University of Waterloo
Waterloo, Ontario

On May 14-16, 1985, the University of Waterloo and the International Development Research Centre (IDRC) held a conference at the University on *Research for Third World Development: Ontario Perspectives*. Basically the objectives were: to identify research priorities; to match Third World needs with Canadian capabilities; and to examine critically existing institutions, programs and processes for cooperation. The overall goal was to overcome constraints, and to explore the feasibility, where warranted, of more effective institutional mechanisms for collaboration. The conference was seen as addressing these objectives mainly from the standpoint of IDRC and the universities, private consultants and research institutions in Ontario. But the conference response clearly offered a much wider Canadian and global perspective.

The conference was organised around keynote papers, plenary sessions and ten workshops, on topics ranging from resources and environment, agricultural research and the rural development process, urbanisation, migration and urban development through others bearing on energy, disease, institutions, information, planning and evaluation, human resources, and scholarly publishing. Details on many aspects of the program are available in *Research for Third World Development: Ontario Perspectives* edited by Len Gertler, University of Waterloo, 1985.

In this publication we are presenting the results of one part of the conference: *The Resources and Environment Workshop*. We are doing this for several reasons. First, as with all workshops, many of the papers and other material could only be **summarised** in the overall conference proceedings. Second, the materials in the Resources and Environment Workshop proved to be unusually rich, in part as a result of the process we used.

In organising interest and participation in the workshop we employed an interactive process, which will be more fully understood when the first paper in the Proceedings, the Workshop Overview, is studied by the reader. We collected a list of likely university faculty, private consultants, and other parties and wrote to them, explaining general plans and inviting ideas and involvement. We received numerous responses from about half of the target group. We then involved many respondents in preparation of brief written contributions relating to resource and environment in Third World development. In consultation with IDRC we also arranged for preparation of some major background papers for the workshop.

SUMMARY OF MAJOR PAPERS AND BRIEF CONTRIBUTIONS

Following the conference all the major background papers and brief written contributions were sent to authors for review and editing. Most changes were minor and the documents are generally published here as they were prepared for the workshop.

The titles of the major papers are:

1. Ontario Research, Resources and Environment in the Third World: A Workshop Introduction and Overview. Nelson, J.G. and Knight, K.D. (University of Waterloo).
2. Research Issues and Directions in Resources and Environment in the Third World. Cecil, R. (University of Western Ontario).
3. Research Priorities for Planning Water Resource Development. Jayal, N.D. (Institute for Ecology Research and Environment Management, New Delhi, India).
4. Local Resources for a Human Environment. Vicencio, R. (International Development Research Centre, Ottawa).

In addition to outlining the rationale and development of the workshop, the overview paper by Nelson and Knight highlighted relevant topics. These included: comprehensive approaches to environmental management; impact assessment; land use and resource classification systems; methods of public involvement; and ethical principles for the conduct of research in the Third World.

Cecil's paper suggested that the identification of research issues and directions in the Third World be considered in the context of two "models", one being comprehensive and rational and the other more indicative of the imperfect knowledge of human conditions in the Third World. In addition, some priorities were suggested to enhance

Canada's participation in Third World research, for example the establishment of research centres and training requirements.

Nalni Jayal focused on current problems with water resource projects in the developing countries, notably in India. In spite of increasing investments in this sector, the temperate, departmental, and engineering biases in water management projects have resulted in a decrease in water supply in several parts of the Third World. Jayal noted that potential areas exist for research in water resource development in the tropics; however, gaps in scientific knowledge need to be addressed, particularly in testing the cost-effectiveness of ecological approaches to water conservation and development.

The paper by Vicencio outlined a policy of concentrating on the development of those resources for which there are local sources and markets. Local resources were considered as being accessible to local populations and requiring a relatively small technical and capital input. It was proposed that the arsenal of modern technology be applied to these neglected resources particularly water, structural materials and nonmetallic minerals.

The titles of the brief written contributions are listed in the Table of Contents. As noted earlier these brief contributions were volunteered by persons who expressed an interest in the workshop after receiving an explanatory letter and an invitation from us. The topics covered by the contributors are quite varied. They range from geology, remote sensing and resource inventory, including archaeology, to eutrophication, fish and water management, waste disposal, energy, landscape design, urbanisation, planning and institutional arrangements.

Many of these brief contributions were sent out in advance of the workshop, along with most of the major background papers. In the next section the discussions and results of the workshop are summarised briefly, followed by the publication of the major background papers and brief written contributions.

WORKSHOP DISCUSSION AND RESULTS

Thirty workshop participants[1] from various universities and research centres discussed the foregoing papers and other ideas pertinent to resources and environment in the Third World. The workshop took place over a two day period. In the course of early discussions two main questions arose:

1. What are the research priorities?
2. What mechanisms can be used to foster more effective communication among researchers in the developing and developed world?

To initiate a focus and continuity in the workshop discussions, it was agreed among the participants to divide into working groups covering Technical Aspects; Training Aspects and Participation/Consultation/Institutional Arrangements. The working groups were encouraged to discuss methodologies pertinent to Third World situations and to determine the implications of research for both Ontario (Canada) and developing countries. The participants later convened in a joint meeting to discuss observations presented by the working groups. The following day the participants debated and elaborated on a draft summary workshop report prepared by the rapporteur which later was presented at the final plenary. The following summary highlights and synthesises the salient points discussed in the report and the workshop.

RESEARCH PRIORITIES

It was acknowledged that the task of identifying research issues and directions with respect to resources, environment and development in the Third World was an immense and multidimensional endeavour. Although it was suggested that research priorities should be country and problem specific and oriented towards the betterment of local peoples, considerable attention focused on the **concerns** underlying priority identification. In this

----

[1] The workshop included representatives from universities (22), government (7) and nongovernment organisations (1). A complete list of workshop participants and those providing papers are included on pages 215-218.

regard, it was agreed that the rational order of priorities may be altered by the vested interests of local decision makers and by political considerations at home and abroad. Thus, Ontario's involvement in Third World research requires being aware of two possible sets of research and development priorities; those dictated by *ecological conditions* and those dictated by *social and political conditions*.

An overriding research priority addressed by the participants was the requirement for a *broader ecological awareness and understanding of environmental problems* in the Third World, particularly in water resource projects. The overreliance on pure engineering alternatives (large dam projects) and sectoral approaches to water resources management have created serious social and ecological instabilities (community displacement, deforestation and flooding) throughout the Third World. The interdependence of soil, biota, and water are not understood or integrated into water management plans. Consequently, it was suggested that more research is required to explore ecological rather than pure engineering alternatives for water resource development in the Third World. In this regard, it was strongly recommended that more *multi- and interdisciplinary approaches* be incorporated into research on *comprehensive water management projects*, particularly in India, Sahel, Haiti and northeast Brazil.

Ontario's research community was seen as having considerable expertise in various integrated and comprehensive methodologies appropriate to diverse Third World resource and development problems. Indeed many Canadian areas share similar problems with developing countries with respect to sparse or nonexistent baseline research on resources. Ontario's experience in the development of new methodologies that require limited data bases can be applied to developing countries for effective decision making and planning purposes. Examples are remote sensing, geographic information systems and flood forecasting.

Other research strengths have been established in:

1.   earth sciences and associated processes;
2.   coastal and freshwater lake development and conservation;
3.   water resources and hydrological processes;
4.   flooding, toxic and other natural and "man-made" hazards;
5.   land use, resource and environmental inventory;
6.   impact evaluation studies;
7.   landscape rehabilitation;
8.   urban ecosystem studies; and
9.   small scale energy studies.

How relevant this expertise is to the needs of developing countries is something that must be continually assessed. Related to this, discussion focused on the need for selecting *research design* strategies in a Third World context, particularly when utilising western based methodologies and technologies. Examples were cited where massive data inventories were completed with little attention given to their eventual application. Consequently, large amounts of time and resources were committed, with only a fraction of the results being utilised. Due to the limited technical and financial resources in developing countries, it is essential that ample lead time should be given to selecting the proper methodology and making the best use of data already collected. A systematic procedure should be followed whereby projects are evaluated in terms of attained goals and objectives and successful implementation and dissemination of results for specific Third World requirements.

Another research priority was identification of *appropriate technologies* and their positive and negative effects when transferred to the Third World. Depending on local circumstances, appropriate technologies can be viewed at any level of sophistication such as simple hand pumps for local peoples or highly technical computer hardware utilised for remote sensing purposes.

In order to implement successfully small scale, locally oriented technology transfer, it was stressed that *researchers must become culturally attuned to the local needs, customs, politics and institutional arrangements of local peoples*.

Thus appropriate technology transfer can be achieved through *shared management responsibility* and close partnership ties in research. Close coordination of infrastructure support and training components is critical for long term success in technology transfer.

Another important research priority was the need to develop projects based on local resources and markets. The rationale for *selecting local areas for development* was to try and maximise the likelihood that the results will directly benefit the poorest sectors of society. Building on this proposal it was recommended that interdisciplinary research teams work closely with local people to implement local level programs properly. Furthermore, it was strongly recommended that researchers *incorporate indigenous knowledge and technology* into local programs. The integration of local needs, talents and technology would also facilitate the adoption of new technologies as well.

MECHANISMS FOR TRAINING AND COMMUNICATION LINKS

A consensus developed among the workshop participants that more attention should be given to fostering closer *collaborative and communicative links* among researchers in the developed and developing world. The proper implementation of any research program involves close networking among researchers to identify research priorities, carry out studies and finally evaluate the success of these activities.

Ontario's capacity to participate in research projects in the Third World could be improved if an organisation such as IDRC established for each developing country or region, a *centralised research documentation centre*. Such a centre could act as a clearing house for research projects and researchers. It would also house relevant publications, identify research needs and foster closer collaborative links among researchers. It would also facilitate Third World researchers working on their own national research programs. In a broader context, such a centre would be useful in disseminating research information. For example, it was pointed out that directories and data bases on research information and expertise exist, but are not known to individual researchers on a systematic centralised basis.

To foster a long term commitment to research, several suggestions were made pertaining to *training of Third World researchers*. In this regard considerable importance was placed on the training of Third World graduate students. Strong support was offered for a three to four month academic and social *acclimatisation period* for Third World students beginning studies in Canada. It was felt that incoming students were initially under undue pressure to perform academically without a proper lead time to adjust either scholastically or socially. The acclimatisation period should be funded and built into all training programs. Strong support was also offered for the development of better *infrastructures* for Third World students in Canada such as improved staffing and supervisory arrangements at universities. A major hindrance to the development of long term research links is the current differential fee structure for foreign students studying in Canada. It was recommended that this arrangement be eliminated.

On the other hand, there should be increased opportunities for *Canadian university students to acquire Third World experience*. IDRC should also create training programs for young Canadian technical experts to become acclimatised to the local and political realities in countries where they intend to do research over the long term. One aim here is to gain cultural and environmental knowledge as well as expertise in a technical specialty within a given country. In all cases, training in multidisciplinary and interdisciplinary approaches was stressed, particularly with a focus on understanding the socio-economic impacts of resource and environment development projects in the Third World.

It was also suggested that IDRC and other international funding agencies finance the *establishment of environmental research and training institutes in developing countries*. Environmental institutes such as the one in Khartoum reportedly have been cost-effective and mutually beneficial to researchers in the developed as well as the developing world, especially in facilitating faculty exchange and technology transfer. In addition, it was recommended that IDRC should provide *funding for the training of nationals in their home country* when involved in indigenous research projects. In order to formulate future research issues and directions properly, it was recommended that IDRC *evaluate* the results of various *training programs* of the past fifteen years and disseminate the findings to interested parties.

More *regular meetings between Ontario and Third World institutions* should be promoted to create greater familiarity with research conditions and requirements and to facilitate faculty/student exchanges. Any mechanisms to facilitate this process such as more workshops, seminars, conferences, exchanges and training programs would be welcomed and provide valuable experience for better networking and more effective collaborative research programs in the future.

PART I

MAJOR BACKGROUND PAPERS

CHAPTER 1

ONTARIO RESEARCH, RESOURCES AND ENVIRONMENT IN THE THIRD WORLD: A WORKSHOP INTRODUCTION AND OVERVIEW

J.G. Nelson
and
K. Drew Knight
Faculty of Environmental Studies
University of Waterloo
Waterloo, Ontario

BACKGROUND AND ORGANISATION OF THE RESOURCES AND ENVIRONMENT WORKSHOP

Two concerns underlie this workshop and its focus on technical and economic approaches to resources and environment in the Third World. The first is the achievement of greater well being among Third World peoples through wiser use of resources and environment. The second is to determine how research can contribute more effectively to this process, particularly research conducted in universities and comparable institutions in Ontario. Such research would be undertaken with full awareness that in spite of many worthwhile efforts in the past, it is necessary to do better in the future for the reasons stated below:

- Enormously large numbers of people - 3.8 billion or 77 per cent of the world population in 1981 - are in Third World situations, characterised by relatively low industrial development, low capital resources, low literacy rates and poor health conditions.

- Third World countries have been involved in the last three decades in a style of development which has not only given rise to serious economic difficulties and high foreign indebtedness, but also resulted in significant deterioration in environmental quality.
- The 1972 Stockholm and subsequent "environmental" conferences have resulted in improvements in ideas, policies, and practices but two major shortcomings have become evident; a sectoral view of man, resources, and environment and a negative approach to solutions.
- With respect to the sectoral view; mining, farming, water, soils, forestry, and other sectors still tend to be studied and dealt with separately.
- The negative approach is apparent at the broad conceptual level where development and environment have been viewed as opposing concerns.
- The 1980 international World Conservation Strategy (WCS) with its stress on positive links between development and conservation is helpful in this regard, as is the associated concept of sustainable development.
- Research applicable to Third World problems has often been carried on in a narrow fashion, without the contact among disciplines needed to provide a comprehensive understanding of development and its effect upon the human and natural environments.
- More multidisciplinary and interdisciplinary approaches are seen as desirable.
- Large scale developments have not been planned and managed in sufficiently close contact with affected local people.
- Given the experience of the last two decades, Third Worlders tend to be less attracted by general development theories.
- Third Worlders now tend to view economic problems against the background of indigenous resource endowments, institutions, and management capabilities.
- Developed countries offer research and expertise to the Third World at some risk of poor fit and malfunction, and also in the knowledge that many Third World type problems have persisted for many decades at home.
- Behind all this also is uncertainty about what constitutes the good life and what role an outsider has in defining it. See, for example, Gertler *et al.*, (1984); Howard-Clinton (1984); Mabogunje (1984); Rees (1984) and various papers in *Ambio*. (1984) for an elaboration on these points.

In light of the foregoing considerations, it was decided to approach the question of what Ontario universities and research institutions could offer to the Third World by structuring the workshop around studies undertaken in the Third World itself and in parts of the so called developed countries which are comparable to the Third World, for example, Canada's North. Other research would also be of interest if a methodology were especially applicable to Third World issues.

In early discussions with the International Development Research Centre (IDRC), stress was placed on interest in earth science topics as these constituted the major part of their new resources program. This interest was linked with the more general concerns discussed previously through the following proposed Resources and Environment workshop themes:

1. earth sciences and associated processes and resources;
2. water resources and hydrological processes;
3. flooding, toxic, and other natural and artificial hazards;
4. land use and/or resource and environmental inventory and classifications;
5. coastal and fresh water lake development and conservation; and
6. impact evaluation studies, and planning and management concerns.

The foregoing themes were circulated in a November 15, 1984, letter, to about fifty knowledgeable persons in industry, the private sector, and government. About twenty replies were received as of January 7, 1985, with the great proportion from universities and government. Several suggestions were made, for example, that climatic change and institutional arrangements should receive more attention, and that archaeological resources might be treated as an aspect of earth science research. On January 15, 1985, a second letter, with some changes in the themes and program, was sent to twenty-two respondents. The current document is the third circular and constitutes an overview paper for the workshop.

It is proposed that the six themes remain as originally suggested, but they will be treated in different ways. Some will be highlighted in *major background papers*; examples are topics relating to water use and management. Others will be referred to in *brief written contributions* volunteered by participants who responded to our circular letters and expressed an interest in presenting ideas to the workshop. In addition the following topics were suggested as having potential application to Third World resource issues and were intended to stimulate workshop discussions.

COMPREHENSIVE APPROACHES TO ENVIRONMENTAL MANAGEMENT

Management Assessment Framework

Figure 1 portrays the type of analytical framework which can be used to assess the comprehensiveness of development and environmental management programs and projects. In this case "management" is taken to include aspects ranging from the agencies or actors involved and their legal or other mandates, through planning, implementation, and general guides or characteristics of the system. The analytical framework is hierarchical. It can be extended to include additional detail and take into account more theory and experience in different disciplines and fields of study. Thus, seven categories of planning are included at the second level. These can be broken down still further if desired. For example, under "strategic planning" could be included goals, objectives, criteria for judging performance, and conceptual and philosophical matters.

Such analytical frameworks can serve as useful planning guides for programs or projects. They are also useful in identifying weaknesses and strengths in planning and management systems and as guides for research and evaluation studies. In the latter respect, monitoring and post-hoc assessment of the effectiveness of projects - of the extent to which goals were achieved - are most important in respect of future planning and sound management (see Gertler *et al.*, 1984, various papers). Many aspects of the comprehensive planning and management approach represented by the model are related to themes for this workshop. Further research on comprehensive management frameworks and approaches is desirable in Third World contexts.

Other	Industry	New Agency	Committee Commission	International Federal	Provincial	Local	Government or Management Level or Type	
								AGENCY
							Lead Agency	
							Participating Agency	
							Strategic Planning	PLANNING
							Forecasting	
							Inventory Biophysical & Social)	
							Land Classification	
							Especially Significant Areas	
							Evaluation	
							Design	
							Negotiated Development — Approval	IMPLEMENTATION
							Pre-Hearing	
							Hearing	
							Formal Case Record	
							Permit Order with Conditions	
							Appeals	
							Final Decision	
							Surveillance & Inspection — Construction and Operation	
							Monitoring	
							Enforcement	
							Modification	
							Research	GENERAL GUIDES OR CHARACTERISTICS
							Government — Co-ordination	
							Industry	
							Public	
							Inter-group	
							Economic Incentives	
							Information Access	
							Management Process Monitoring	
								COMMENTS

Source: Nelson and Jessen (1984)

Figure 1: Management Assessment Model (revised)

Conceptual Ecological Modelling

Another comprehensive approach in environmental management and assessment involves conceptual ecological modelling. One such modelling methodology developed by Odum (1983) as illustrated in Figure 2 provides a graphical framework for organising and interpreting interactions among resources, energy sources, biophysical processes, material and energy flow pathways and cultural stresses within complex ecological systems. Interaction matrices developed from graph theory (Harary *et al.*, 1965) can be integrated with ecological models to calculate and chart interdependent relationships among components that are not readily apparent in the models; for example, food chains and stress pathways (Knight, 1983; Knight *et al.*, 1984).

An integrated model/matrix approach can be utilised as a precondition for resource planning and environmental impact assessments by defining problems, establishing ecological boundaries, and integrating information for an initial qualitative understanding of the structure and function of ecosystems. In addition, the modelling process facilitates an interdisciplinary approach to problem solving and communication among researchers. Indeed, conceptual modelling has been a widely recognised and extensively used tool among ecologists, resource planners and managers, particularly in characterising complex coastal ecosystems for planning purposes (Clark, 1977; Woodruff *et al.*, 1978), guiding ecosystem management oriented research (Francis *et al.*, 1985), and directing impact assessments (Beanlands and Duinker, 1983; Gilliland and Risser, 1977; Knight, 1983; Tornebohm, 1984; Walker and Norton, 1982; Wang *et al.*, 1980; and various papers in Hall and Day, 1977). In addition, conceptual modelling techniques offer the advantage of a preliminary ecological "scoping" exercise prior to the more expensive simulation and mathematical modelling packages used in environmental assessment. This approach would minimise the possibility of overlooking key impacts.

Conceptual modelling techniques seem appropriate for an initial understanding of many of the complex interactions of ecosystems in the Third World, such as tropical rain forests, mangrove swamps, and coral reefs. However, several limitations are inherent with such an approach and must be taken into account in determining the operational utility of conceptual modelling tools. They include problems with familiarisation and costs of "new" techniques, the identification of impacts, the need for baseline data and issues concerning a balance between complexity and simplification in the modelling process.

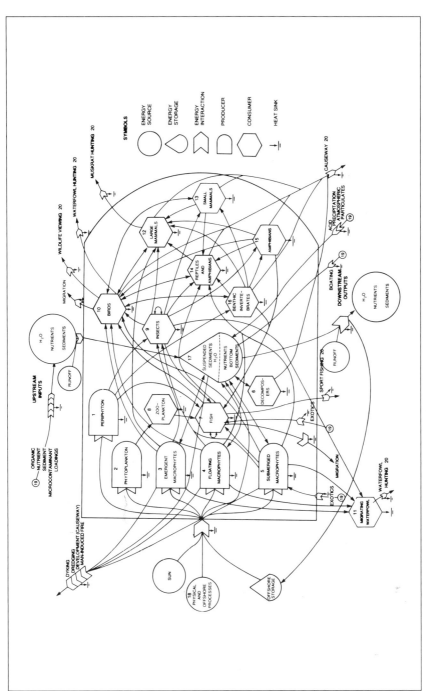

Figure 2: Conceptual Ecological Model of a Grassy Marsh Community – Long Point Ecosystem

APPROACHES TO IMPACT EVALUATION STUDIES

Impact evaluation studies often termed Environmental Impact Assessment (EIA) can lead to a broad view of the unwanted social and environmental effects as well as means of mitigating or avoiding them. It has also been contended that such assessments can work in favour of development, tending to facilitate it, overriding local concerns and wishes.

Some very useful work in EIA, in the broad sense of the term, where a wide array of socio-economic and biophysical factors and effects are included, has been completed by the Project Appraisal for Development Control Unit (PADC) at Aberdeen University. PADC also has organised short courses and other assistance to government, corporate, and other personnel interested in EIA. The PADC people have tried to develop an EIA approach that is relatively economical and efficient and which can be built into a planning and management process.

Figure 3 graphically summarises the major components of the assessment process as practiced by PADC (Tomlinson, 1984). Research on the strengths, weaknesses, and improvements required in EIA methods applicable in Third World contexts are very desirable and a number of Ontario universities have the necessary skills and experience. Examples and discussions of various approaches to EIA by Ontario researchers, including the social and technical aspects, can be found in the Ministry of the Environment, *EA update* and in Mitchell (1979), Newkirk (1979), and Whitney and MacLaren (1985). Other recent reviews of EIA techniques and methodologies can be referenced in Beanlands and Duinker (1983), Lee (1982), Nichols and Hyman (1982), Shopley and Fuggle (1984), and in *EIA Review*.

LAND USE AND RESOURCE CLASSIFICATION SYSTEMS

Many of the Third World problems require information on ecosystems, resources, land characteristics, or other attributes of the environment proposed for development. Such information is fundamentally useful in linking proposed uses with appropriate lands and avoiding loss of good agricultural soils, flood plains, critical wildlife habitats, arid or other hazard areas, and other life support systems.

Largely as a result of concern over limited availability of agricultural land, Canadians have been very active in the development and use of land and resource classification systems, over fifty of which

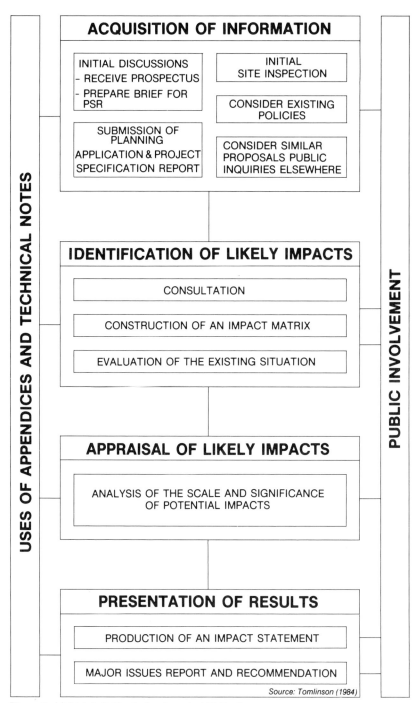

Figure 3: Linked Activities in the Appraisal Method

are outlined in *Land Use Classification Systems: An Overview* (Scace, 1981) and others in Petch (1984). These systems frequently have similar characteristics but there also are important distinctions among them. Many of them are also applicable to remote sensing techniques which will be addressed by Dr. Pala in a brief written contribution (see Chapter 9) to this Workshop.

The Canada Land Inventory, which was conducted throughout the country in the 1950s is largely based on the notion of capability to produce certain resources on a sustainable basis (Canada, Environment Canada, 1978). It has been computerised by Lands Directorate personnel of the federal Department of the Environment in the form of the Canada Land Data System (Thie *et al.*, 1982).

The Ecological Land Classification system is largely intended to identify a wide range of abiotic (geologic) and biotic factors at work in the environment, and synthesise these into aggregate maps at a number of different scales or levels such as the ecoregion (1:1,000,000), ecodistrict (1:250,000) and ecosite (1:150,000) (Wicken, 1981). This Ecological Land Classification (ELC) system can also be computerised. In addition, ELC activity at the Lands Directorate, Department of Environment, Ottawa, has resulted in mapping applications with respect to Third World problems, particularly in North Africa.

Other mapping methodologies include the ABC or abiotic, biotic, and cultural resource classification system which is intended to provide information on the biophysical and the human aspects of an urban or rural environment (Dorney and Hoffman, 1979). In other words, it attempts to integrate natural and cultural information. A variation of the ABC system has recently been developed for a particular use in environmentally significant areas (ESA) in the Canadian North (Grigoriew *et al.*, 1985). It attempts to integrate abiotic, biotic, land use and cultural information and links these data to appropriate institutional arrangements such as parks, wildlife and other management areas. A computerised basis for this system has also been recently developed (Smith, 1984).

In selecting among available systems, or in developing new or modified versions for Third World use, careful attention should be paid to the following factors: the goals and objectives of the classification exercise; the cost of applying the system; efficiency, complexity, and training requirements; ease of aggregation and disaggregation of the data for use for different purposes; ease of interrelating biophysical, land use and management considerations; adaptability to both manual and computer use, usefulness in EIA and other program and project evaluation exercises; and comprehensibility to lay users.

METHODS OF PUBLIC INVOLVEMENT

Although public involvement procedures theoretically are as worthwhile in the Third World as in more developed contexts, they have been used less for a variety of well known reasons. Language, institutional, and other barriers face those attempting to assess local and regional reactions to development concepts, programs and projects. Nevertheless, many methods of involvement are available as show in Tables 1 and 2 and have characteristics which make them adaptable to a variety of social and environmental situations (Sadler, 1977). These approaches have largely been applied in developed areas. Many of them have been used successfully in planning and managing oil and gas or other development projects in the Canadian North, frequently with positive results from the standpoint of indigenous people and other interested parties (Berger, 1977; Federal Environmental Assessment Review Office, 1985). Such methods should be studied and considered for use in terms of the array of contexts that characterises the Third World.

ETHICAL PRINCIPLES FOR THE CONDUCT OF RESEARCH IN THE THIRD WORLD

Underlying any research relating to development is the matter of ethics (Mitchell and Draper, 1982). This is particularly the case in Third World contexts, where people in the past often have not been properly informed or involved in research directly or indirectly affecting their well being. In Canada, such situations have been addressed by the Association of Canadian Universities for Northern Studies (ACUNS) in the context of its concern for research in the Canadian North. Northerners have been seen as involved in research in several different ways: (1) as research subjects; (2) providing information; (3) as part of a research team; (4) using the completed research; (5) identifying research needs. The following principles have been advanced by ACUNS (1982) for northern research:

1. The research must respect the privacy and dignity of the people.
2. The research should take into account the knowledge and experience of the people.
3. The research should respect the language, traditions and standards of the community.

Table 1

Stages and Techniques in a Citizen Participation Program
A Comparative Summary

Cooperative   Confronting
Government Agency   Citizen Organization

Start-up

Cooperative Government Agency	Confronting Citizen Organization
1. Review of Recent Events	1. Review of Agency and Project
2. Visits to Key People	2. Visits to Key People
3. Participation Program Design	3. Participation Program Design
4. Staffing	4. Organizing Volunteers
5. Introductory Brochure	5. Alerting Flyer
6. Politial Preview	6. Mass Media
7. Mass Media	7. Confrontation
8. Open House	

Collecting Information

9. Personal Observation	8. Personal Observation
10. Key Information Sources	9. Key Information Sources
11. Joint Planning	10. Monitoring
12. Meetings with Groups	11. Community Self-Survey
13. Resource People	12. Meetings with Groups
14. Schools	13. Joint Planning
	14. Resource People
	15. Schools

Mutual Education

15. Information Output	16. Information Output
16. Evaluation Factors Checklist	17. Distribution of Information
17. Political Preview	18. Open House
18. Distribution of Information	19. Joint Planning
19. Open House	20. Meetings with Groups
20. Joint Planning	21. Resource People
21. Meetings with Groups	22. Schools
22. Resource People	23. Feedback
23. Schools	24. Workshops
24. Feedback	25. Reference Centre
25. Workshops	
26. Reference Centres	

Public Preferences

27. Information Output	26. Information Output
28. Mass Media Campaign	27. Mass Media
29. Political Preview	28. Citizen Leaders Meeting
30. Citizen Leaders Meeting	29. Open House
31. Open House	30. Tabulation of Responses
32. Tabulation of Responses	31. Public Meetings or Hearings
33. Contribution to Final Report	

Decision and Follow-Up

34. Presentation to Elected Representatives
35. Conveying Decision to Citizens
36. Linking to Implementation
37. Evaluation

Source: Sadler (1977)

Table 2

Catalog of Techniques

1. Advocacy Planning
2. Arbitrative and Mediative Planning
3. Charrette
4. Citizens' Advisory Committee
5. Citizen Employment
6. Citizen Honoraria
7. Citizen Referendum
8. Citizen Representatives on Public Policy-making Bodies
9. Citizen Review Board
10. Citizen Training
11. Community Planning Centre
12. Community Technical Assistance
13. Computer-based Techniques Teleconferencing, Polling, Games, Interactive Graphics
14. Co-ordinator or Co-ordinator-Catalyst
15. Design-in and Colour Mapping
16. Drop-in Centres
17. Fishbowl Planning
18. Game Simulation
19. Group Dynamics Conflict Utilization Opinionaire, Empathy, Feedback, Relations Diagramming, Video-Taped Group Interview, Brainstorming, Force Field Analysis, Nominal Group Process, Role Play, Synetics, Thurst Problem Analysis

20. Hotline
21. Interactive Cable TV-Based Participation
22. Media-Based Issue Balloting
23. Meetings – Community-sponsored
24. Meetings – Neighbourhood
25. Meetings – Open Information
26. Neighbourhood Planning Council
27. Ombudsman
28. Plural Planning
29. Policy Capturing
30. Public Hearing
31. Public Information Programs
32. Task Force
33. Value Analysis
34. Workshops
35. Delphi
36. Focused Group Discussions
37. Survey of Citizens' Attitudes and Opinions

Source: Sadler (1977)

4.   The person in charge of the research is accountable for all decisions on the project, including the decisions of subordinates.
5.   No research should begin before being fully explained to those who might be affected.
6.   No research should begin without the consent of those who might be affected.
7.   In seeking informed consent, researchers should clearly identify sponsors, purposes of the research, sources of financial support, and investigators responsible for the research.
8.   In seeking informed consent, researchers should explain the potential effects of the research on the community and the environment.
9.   Informed consent should be obtained from each participant in research, as well as from the community at large.
10. Participants should be fully informed of any data gathering techniques to be used (tape and video recordings, photos, physiological measures, etc.), and the use to which they will be put.
11. No undue pressure should be applied to get consent for participation in a research project.
12. Research subjects should remain anonymous unless they have agreed to be identified; if anonymity cannot be guaranteed, the subject must be informed of the possible consequences of this before becoming involved in the research.
13. If, during the research, the community decides that the research may be unacceptable to the community, the researcher and the sponsor should suspend the study.
14. Ongoing explanations of research objectives, methods, findings and their interpretation should be made available to the community, with the opportunity for the people to comment before publication; summaries should also be made available in the local language.
15. Subject to requirements for anonymity, descriptions of the data should be left on file on the communities from which it was gathered, along with descriptions of the methods used and the place of data storage.
16. All research reports should be sent to the communities involved.
17. All research publications should refer to informed consent and community participation.

18.   Subject to requirements for anonymity, publications should give appropriate credit to everyone who contributes to the research.

REFERENCES

Ambio, (1984) *Population, Resources and Environment*, XIII(3).

Association of Canadian Universities for Northern Studies (1982) *Ethical Principles for the Conduct of Research in the North*, Ottawa, Occasional Paper No. 7.

Bastedo, J.D., Nelson, J.G. and Theberge, J.B. (1984) "Ecological approach to resource survey and planning for environmentally significant areas: the ABC method," *Environmental Management*, 8(2): 125-34.

Beanlands, G.E. and Duinker, P.N. (1983) *An Ecological Framework for Environmental Impact Assessment in Canada*, Halifax: Dalhousie University, Institute for Resource and Environmental Studies.

Berger, T.R. (1977) *Northern Frontier Northern Homeland. The Report of the Mackenzie Valley Pipeline Inquiry*, Vols. I and II, Ottawa: Supply and Services Canada.

Biswas, M.R. and Biswas, A.K. (1982) "Environment and sustained development in the Third World: a review of the past decade," *Third World Quarterly*, 4(4): 479-91.

Canada, Environment Canada (1978) *The Canada Land Inventory: Objectives, Scope and Organisation*, Ottawa: Lands Directorate, Environment Canada, Canada Land Inventory Report No. 1 (revised).

Clark, J. (1977) *Coastal Ecosystem Management*, New York: John Wiley and Sons.

Dorney, R.S. and Hoffman, D.W. (1979) "Development of landscape planning concepts and management strategies for an urbanising agricultural region," *Landscape Planning*, 6: 151-77.

Federal Environmental Assessment Review Office (1985) *Register of Panel Projects*, No. 22.

Francis, G.R., Grima, A.P.L., Regier, H.A. and Whillans, T.H. (1985) *A Prospectus for the Management of the Long Point Ecosystem*, Ann Arbor, Michigan: Great Lakes Fishery Commission Technical Report No. 43.

Gertler, L., Bennett, K. and Levitt, K. (eds.) (1984) *Environments*, 16:(3).

Gilliland, M.W. and Risser, P.G. (1977) "The use of systems diagrams for environmental impact assessment: procedures and an application," *Ecological Modelling*, 3: 183-209.

Grigoriew, P., Theberge, J.B. and Nelson, J.G. (1985) *Park Boundary Delineation Manual, The ABC Resource Survey Approach*, Waterloo: University of Waterloo, Heritage Resources Centre.

Hall, C.A.S. and Day, J.W. (eds.) (1977) *Ecosystem Modelling in Theory and Practice*, New York: John Wiley and Sons.

Harary, R., Norman, R.Z. and Chartwright, D. (1965) *Structural Models: An Introduction to the Theory of Directed Graphs*, New York: John Wiley and Sons.

Howard-Clinton, E.G. (1984) "The emerging concepts of environmental issues in Africa," *Environmental Management*, 8(3): 187-90.

Knight, K.D. (1983) "Conceptual ecological modelling and interaction matrices as environmental assessment tools with reference to the Long Point ecosystem, Lake Erie," Waterloo: University of Waterloo, Department of Geography, unpublished M.A. thesis.

Knight, K.D., Dufournaud, C. and Mulamoottil, G. (1984) "Conceptual ecological modelling and interaction matrices as environmental assessment tools in coastal planning," *Water Science and Technology*, 16: 559-67.

Lee, N. (1982) "The future development of environmental impact assessment," *Environmental Management*, 14: 71-90.

Mabogunje, A.L. (1984) "The poor shall inherit the earth: issues of environmental quality and Third World development," *Geoforum*, 15(3): 295-306.

Ministry of the Environment. *EA Update*, Toronto, Ministry of the Environment.

Mitchell, B. (1979) *Geography and Resource Analysis*, London: Longman Group Limited.

Mitchell, B. and Draper, D. (1982) *Relevance and Ethics in Geography*, Burnt Mill: Longman Group Limited.

Nelson, J.G. and Jessen, S. (1984) *Planning and Managing Environmentally Significant Areas in the Northwest Territories: Issues and Alternatives*, Ottawa: Canadian Arctic Resources Committee, University of Waterloo.

Newkirk, R.T. (1979) *Environmental Planning for Utility Corridors*, Ann Arbor, Michigan: Ann Arbor Science.

Nichols, R. and Hyman, E. (1982) "Evaluation of environmental assessment methods," *Journal of the Water Resources Planning and Management Division*, 108: 87-105.

Odum, H.T. (1983) *Systems Ecology: An Introduction*, New York: John Wiley and Sons.

Petch, A. (ed.) (1984) *Lands Directorate Publications*, Ottawa, Lands Directorate.

Rees, J.A. (1984) "Environmental quality issues in the 1980s: an overview," *Geoforum*, 15(3): 287-93.

Sadler, B. (ed.) (1977) *Involvement and Environment*, Proceedings of the Canadian Conference on Public Participation, Vol. 1, Banff, Alberta, Environment Council of Alberta.

Scace, R.C. (1981) *Land Use Classification System: An Overview*, Ottawa: Lands Directorate, Environment Canada, Working Paper No. 14.

Shopley, J.B. and Fuggle, R.F. (1984) "A comprehensive review of current environmental impact assessment methods and techniques," *Environmental Management*, 18: 25-47.

Smith, P.G.R. (1984) "Identifying and evaluating environmentally significant areas in the Northwest Territories: a review, a proposed evaluation system and a test application," Waterloo: University of Waterloo, School of Urban and Regional Planning, unpublished M.A. thesis.

Thie, J., Switzer, W.A. and Chartrand, N. (1982) "The Canada land data system and its applications to landscape planning and resource management." Paper presented at the International Symposium on Landscape Information Systems, Wissenschaftszentrum, Bonn-Bad Godesberg.

Tomlinson, P. (1984) "The assessment of industrial development: methodologies and experiences," *Environments*, 16(3): 77-78.

Tornebohm, E. (1984) "Conceptual ecological modelling and energy analysis as applied to Keswick Marsh, Ontario," Waterloo: University of Waterloo, Department of Geography, unpublished M.A. Research Paper.

Walker, H. and Norton, G.A. (1982) "Applied ecology: towards a positive approach: II. Applied ecological analysis," *Environmental Management*, 14(4): 325-40.

Wang, F.C., Odum, H.T. and Kangas, R.C. (1980) "Energy analysis for environmental impact assessment," *Journal of the Water Resources Planning and Management Division*, (July): 451-66.

Wicken, E.B. (1981) *Ecological Land Classification: Analysis and Methodologies*, Lands Directorate, Ecological Land Classification Series, No. 6.

Whitney, J.B.R. and MacLaren, V.W. (1985) *Environmental Impact Assessment: The Canadian Experiences*, Toronto: University of Toronto, Institute of Environmental Studies.

Woodruff, C.M., Longley, W.L. and Reed, A.E. (1978) "Inland boundary determination for coastal management purposes: an ecological systems approach to requirements of the Federal Coastal Zone Management Act of 1972," *Coastal Zone Management Journal*, 4: 189-211.

CHAPTER 2

RESEARCH ISSUES AND DIRECTIONS IN RESOURCES AND ENVIRONMENT IN THE THIRD WORLD

Robert G. Cecil
Department of Geography
University of Western Ontario
London, Ontario

Any attempt to identify research issues and directions in resources and environment management in the Third World must first address the realities of the magnitude of the task. Clearly, the dimensions that must be considered are immense. More than 100 countries are involved, each with n number of sets of environmental complexes, needing scrutiny and research, at myriads of scales, involving an almost limitless number of elements and variables. Also, everywhere, assorted research and development projects already are completed or in progress, further complicating the overall situation.

An attempt can be made to set the universe of problems, and their locations, into a manageable framework by proposing generalised models to represent combinations and permutations of key variables that interact under different sets of circumstances, when humans manipulate resources and environments. A first model is proposed that shows an idealised situation, which, it is hoped, most specialists and researchers try to achieve either unconsciously or consciously. However, as logic dictates, the conditions displayed in the model are never even remotely attainable. A second model portrays a totally opposite set of conditions, at the other extreme of the continuum, with emphasis placed on variables that impede the smooth progression of development. Again, an extreme scenario is given, and it is expected that all the detrimental conditions shown would never prevail simultaneously. Moreover, it is assumed that the individual problems shown may not be as accentuated as suggested in the model. Somewhere between the two extremes are the conditions that currently prevail in development research and planning in the Third World.

Conditions vary from location to location, and from time to time, and run the gamut from a close approximation of the problems in the second model, to situations that tend, in part, to reflect some of the desirable elements of Model One. The models are a reminder of the infinite number of permutations and combinations of human environmental elements that confront researchers and planners with an ever changing kaleidoscope of situations. None of the latter should ever reach the extremes portrayed in the models. But, researchers should keep such abstractions in mind as a reminder, on the one hand, of the pitfalls lying in wait, and, on the other hand, of the potential for meaningful analysis if research can be pursued under reasonable and credible conditions. The models are designed not so much for those who already work in the Third World and who are as aware as they can be, but for those who would work and who may not be as aware as they should be.

After the models have been outlined, this paper focusses briefly on some of the major issues concerning Canadian participation in Third World research and development. The latter are raised simply because there are some crucial questions that must be raised when Canadians become involved in the process of planning and management in foreign countries. This paper goes on to document two highly positive projects, prototypes in their own right, that open many avenues for discussion, and then goes on to look at failure and wastage. The focus is then changed to raise the issue of local perception of resources, and of the fundamental problems created by resource abuse at the micro and macro levels. This paper ends with some brief references to precedents in the literature on research issues and development in the Third World, but with a view to raising questions rather than providing answers.

MODEL ONE

Part I of the first model (Appendix A) demands nothing short of full knowledge of the total physical/environmental nature of a country. Nobody is capable of ever approximating such knowledge, but individuals and groups should strive to accumulate as much basic knowledge as possible. It is particularly important that operations at any one location be seen in their areal, regional, national and international contexts, and that relationships between different parts of a country, or countries, be grasped, when projects get underway.

Part II recalls the importance of the human condition. The set of variables used in the model are the obvious ones; there are many others. However, it is not so much the iteration of specific variables that is the concern here; rather, it is the principle that human heterogeneity should be a primary concern of the development planner. The reality of the Third World is that in virtually every country there is the juxtaposition in the same space of at least two cultural groups, often many more. Moreover, human attributes create a wide range of within-group heterogeneity. Consequently, it is difficult to know which people to place within which socio-economic-cultural sets when dealing with specific developmental issues. Yet, such human sets, themselves dynamic as people aggregate and disaggregate in reaction to evolving events, have a great deal of impact in the development process. Therefore, ideally, one should have as vast a knowledge as possible of the inner workings of cultures, and be able to recognise what sets of human groups will have the most impact in the locations where research and development are underway.

Part III of the model sets forth some desirable conditions, a fraction of the possible range, under which research and development should take place. It is a reminder that the motivation of all the people involved in projects is all important. There is an assumption that the more honesty, sincerity, cooperation, and positive interaction among people, the more likely that there will be a genuine concern to better the human condition of the people affected by project implementations.

Part IV suggests that a great deal of thought has to be given to local as well as to national priorities. There is an implication that a great deal of effort should be made to select the best policies and to make meaningful decisions to maximise the positive effects of projects for the largest number of people.

Finally, the last part of the model reminds us of the limitations of any one mind, or any groups of minds. It is also a reminder that no model can cover the universe, and that the basic duty of the research

analyst is to continue to strive to learn, especially in the Third World
as it holds so many unknowns for the foreigner.

MODEL TWO

The second model (Appendix B) focusses on those major
elements of reality that impede research and development in the Third
World. The idea is to suggest a sample of elements that combine the
worst possible scenarios. Any one of the impediments can be serious
enough, but, unfortunately, more often than not, many occur
simultaneously, causing serious problems for research and
development.

The first part of the model shows some of the major problems of
damage and abuse to the environment and to resources in the Third
World. Naturally, the first priority of research and development in
developing countries is to come to grips with these and other similar
problems, i.e. to rehabilitate what has been abused and damaged, and
to protect and preserve that which is still comparatively unscathed.
But, the second part of the model suggests, and practical experience
confirms, that such goals are not easy to pursue or achieve, because
people seem to have an infinite capacity to interfere with each other's
efforts. A summary of the human elements would suggest that
individuals and groups represent the greatest threat to research and
development in the Third World. Specifically, as part four indicates,
conditions for working in the field may be difficult, and may interfere
with a project before, during and after, the fact. Moreover, there is
always a danger that policies will be ill-chosen and that a project might
have a lot of negative effects on the people and regions meant to be
served. Consequently, the question of evaluation must be raised.
Unfortunately, it is a process for which there is no standard
methodology or time frame. Finally, when everything else is
considered, there could be sets of unknown factors that may doom a
project before it sees the light of day.

THE DILEMMA OF PRIORITIES: AN ISSUE

The extremes portrayed in the two models suggest that it would
be impossible to come to an agreement on absolute priorities for
research and development in the Third World. But, the models can
only caution decision makers, who, of necessity, must continue to
make choices. Fortunately, the latter can be made with the assistance

of a huge body of material covering the middle ground. But, not all such material is universally accessible, which is a complicating factor in choosing priorities.

Another complicating factor stems from the actual groups that must make the ultimate decisions on priorities. Ideally, national resource personnel, with or without their foreign colleagues, should be the prime decision makers, but vested interests of such groups on the one hand, and, political considerations at home and abroad, on the other hand, may decidedly alter the rational order of priorities in any one nation.

In reality, there are two possible sets of research and development priorities. The first is the one dictated by political expediency and considerations. The Canadian participant who gets involved in the selection of priorities should be able to have maximum opportunities in Canada to study the relevant human environmental complexes. But, such opportunities are not as readily available as they could be. Therefore, some consideration should be given to enhance the capacity of Canadians to interact more effectively in the Third World, and to that effect, some priorities that are desirable are proposed, even though practical implementation is remote at this stage.

SOME IDEALISED PRIORITIES

It is suggested that Canada's capacity to participate in the selection of research direction and development in the Third World would be improved by the following priorities:

1. Concentration of all pertinent documented information on a depository basis in specified selected locations for each developing country.
2. The recognition of acknowledged experts, both natives and Canadian, on each developing country, and a mechanism to involve such people in virtually all major decision making concerning the country of their particular expertise.
3. The preparation of extensive systems analysis of the ecosystems of each country, if not in whole, at least in part, in order to rationalise the selection of priorities for research and development of the environment and resources.
4. The creation of a training program for Canadian technical experts, who have no Third World experience, in order to sensitise them to the cultural norms and needs of the countries in which they will serve briefly.

CANADIAN RESEARCH CAPACITY: AN ISSUE

There is no doubt that Canada has the capacity to conduct Third World research. But, the perennial question is whether or not that capacity is used effectively. And the answer must be somewhat negative in a general sense, when looking at the way our human resources are distributed, mobilised and used. Looking at the four idealised priorities above, Canada lags behind other developed countries in organising its research capacity, which is an issue that must be addressed prior to articulating Third World research priorities, because the two sets of variables are highly intertwined.

It might be practical and desirable to have in Canada the kind of Third World-oriented research and documentation centres operated in France, by the Centre National de Recherche Scientifique (CNRS). The attractive features of such centres are:

1. An incorporated documentation centre that collects every publication of importance on specified topics on those countries that are deemed to be of specific interest to specific centres.
2. The presence of a dedicated cadre of highly competent full time researchers, working on a narrow range of topics on a long term ongoing basis, with frequent visits to selected small numbers of overseas locations.
3. The availability of long term attachments for visiting researchers.

By the same token, as is well known, France has overseas research centres for its scientific personnel, notably through its network of l'Office de la Recherche Scientifique et Technique d'Outre-Mer (ORSTOM). Nothing in Canada matches such a structure for Third World research, and it should be an issue.

In a similar vein, there are other issues involving Canadian-based researchers that will have to be addressed eventually; they include:

1. The part time research status of most Canadian academics, limiting the time span and the period of the year available for field work.
2. The question of efficiency of individual academics operating independently, using funds obtained from academic funding bodies. When such research is either unsuccessful or not completed, there is a terrible waste of talent, energy and money, not to mention the time of all the nationals who interacted, in one way or another, with the visitors.

3. The need for more coordination and cooperation between permanent development agencies, such as IDRC and CIDA, and the mix of academics who travel back and forth to the Third World.

ISSUES IN THE FIELD

If it is desirable to seek to maximise the efficiency of research capacity in Canada, it is also worthwhile to review a sample of pertinent examples of strengths and weaknesses of the efforts of Canadians, and other researchers, who continue to be involved in the management and the development of resources and their environments in the Third World.

The Las Cuevas Watershed Project in the Dominican Republic: The Issue of Research and Development Continuity

The basic *issues* here[1] involve ecological problems of uncommon magnitude. Essentially, the population is growing, resources are limited, land is poorly distributed and marginally productive steppes are being invaded. So, the resulting ecological problems include accelerated soil erosion, deforestation and downstream sedimentation, with attenuating losses in soil fertility and land productivity, plus alarming reduction in the viability of downstream hydroelectric facilities, which affect the generation of energy and irrigation capacity.

The government of the Dominican Republic recognised that the concept of integrated development was a strategy for dealing with such complex problems and the University of Florida was in an ideal position to provide the expertise to put such a concept into operation at its Center for Latin American Studies. The latter has a complement of full time researchers, one of whom, Dr. Antonini, has over 20 years of continuous professional association with the Dominican Republic. Therefore, he was the logical choice to initiate the project as he was in a position to understand the country's problems from extensive long term, firsthand knowledge, therefore, providing a continuity in ecological-human investigation and development which is rare in Third World research.

----

[1] A full summary of the thrust and direction of the Las Cuevas project is found in Antonini (1981).

Antonini chose one of the country's most affected areas and instituted a large scale, long term research and development project, built on a solid foundation of previous research, and designed to go on, in a sense, almost in perpetuity. The project is a superb example of one of the better ways to mobilise and integrate human resources from a developed and a developing country, and a prototype of the accumulation of the vast amounts of data which Model One suggest are necessary for a successful development project.

The concept of the project is comparatively simple, but rather decisive:

1. It begins by training a substantial number of Dominicans at the Center, at the University of Florida. The trainees are all professionals in their own fields, and are usually at the mid-point in their careers.
2. The Dominicans also train within their own individual disciplines, and are initiated into interdisciplinary team work and research, and they receive instructions in project methodology, design, programming and management.
3. Each trainee must produce a thesis prepared within a systems framework, with field data gathered in the Las Cuevas area.
4. The results of the field work are synthesised and the scientific findings are used to prepare an integrated management and protection plan for the Las Cuevas watershed.

The Las Cuevas project has been ongoing for over five years. Currently, several theses, covering a range of topics,[2] have been completed, and a substantial multivariate data bank has been built up on the watershed. Moreover, and most important, the Las Cuevas watershed project has become a triangle of research and development capacity, involving the University of Florida, the Department of Natural Resources Inventory in the Dominican Republic, and the people in the Las Cuevas watershed. The latter have been an integral part of the research component over the years, and will participate in assorted phases of ecological-economic development that will be introduced and monitored from a research station opening in the area and which will be staffed by individuals with previous research

---

[2] For some samples of recent theses see: Espinal (1983), Reynoso (1983), Nova (1984) and Ledesma (1983).

experience in the area. The latter are part of the country's expanding web of specialists, in many disciplines, who have been trained at Florida. It is almost as though the Center at Florida and the Dominican Republic's Department of Natural Resources Inventory have become an integral whole. Continuity of the project is assured by the core of trained Dominicans, which is being continually augmented. The government now has a strong cadre of scientists able to expand such work into other areas of the country where research on management and development of natural resources is required.

The thrust of the research in the Dominican Republic is most noteworthy. It is planted firmly in systems analysis, and is based on the principles of energy flows through natural ecosystems, and on the relationships of such flows to the human condition. Preliminary work, completed in Florida[3] has created a macro-level land classification scheme for the Dominican Republic. The latter is being used to prepare a micro-level detailed classification of the natural environment in the Dominican Republic, using air photo interpretation, topographic maps and ecological data. Land classes and land capability are then plugged into the overall systems analysis. Appendix C gives a summary on the one hand, of the various subsystems that are being researched, analysed and developed, and, on the other hand, of the specific targets of the development aspects of the project. The analysis is far reaching and detailed, and operates at local, areal and regional scales. The Las Cuevas project is a model of a research direction, and of a system of rationalising the use of personnel, which is well worth emulating in the Third World.

The SCARP Mardan Project in Pakistan: The Issue of Evaluation

The SCARP Mardan Project in Pakistan is providing a development anthropologist at Western, Dr. Freedman, and his Canadian and Pakistani colleagues, with an opportunity, possibly unique on the planet, to undertake a long term, far reaching evaluation of a major Third World development project. Project evaluation is a key issue in resource and environment management in the Third World, and the evaluation project organised and supervised by the Western participants, and to be undertaken through a cooperative arrangement with the Pakistan Academy for Rural Development, may well emerge as the prototype model for all such

----

[3] See Posner, J. *et al.* (1981 and 1983).

evaluation work in the future.

SCARP stands for Salinity Control and Reclamation Project, of which there are a number in place in Pakistan in various stages of implementation. To paraphrase Freedman *et al.*,[4] the SCARP Project at Mardan represents a most important initiative in Pakistan's North-West Frontier. The project at Mardan is a major irrigation, drainage, land reclamation and agricultural development scheme, jointly financed by the International Development Association, CIDA, and the Government of Pakistan. Other Pakistani agencies are involved in the implementation of the project, which is valued at well over 100 million dollars.

The scale of the project is large, and a lot of land area is covered. Therefore, goals are selected to accomplish specific objectives in specified locations. One of the major aims is to increase agricultural production which is intertwined with the provision of irrigation water, but the accompanying increased drainage problems have to be alleviated. The project is involved also with reclaiming land lost to production because of salinity, also with encouraging water use efficiencies, and with upgrading agricultural extension services to area farmers. As Freedman *et al.* point out, a number of major works are to be completed, involving channelisation, drainage, land levelling, land reclamation, agricultural extension, and technical assistance (see details in Appendix D).

In addition to the above major undertakings, CIDA is providing full funding for one additional crucial major component in the project, i.e. for monitoring and evaluating the socio-economic impacts of the environmental management projects. The evaluation is under the direct control of Dr. Freedman, who is undertaking the work with a few Canadian and a larger number of Pakistani colleagues.

The evaluation process is striking in terms of the time span involved, almost a decade. At the outset, a 20 month period was allocated for a first phase of evaluation, which began in January 1984. The first study will set the stage, in terms of data, techniques, and other aspects of evaluation, for a second phase, slated to last 20 months also, and due to begin in mid-1987, and continue into 1989. To quote Freedman *et al.* the purpose of the second phase is:

> to provide a comparison with the data collected during Phase I, in order to account, as accurately as possible, for the impacts of SCARP Mardan along a number of dimensions.

----

[4] The project is fully explained in Freedman, J. *et al.* (1983).

(Freedman *et al.*, 1983)

The dimensions mentioned above are many and varied, with the evaluation team aiming for a most comprehensive review of the resource/environment management project. The dimensions of the evaluation are far ranging and elaborate, and far too numerous and complex to reproduce here. However, a summary of some of the features of the evaluation is given in Appendix D.

One of the major objectives of the evaluation is to gauge the impact of works done under SCARP on farming communities, on individual farms, and on the people who do the actual farming. The evaluation welds the socio-economic component to the environmental-resource management component, gauging how the latter affects the farmer. The evaluation will concentrate on documenting changes in such variables as farm yields and incomes, cropping patterns, resource use, marketing, employment, wealth distribution, and to quote Freedman *et al.* (1983) again: "will examine a number of crucial economic and social patterns which may critically affect the ability of SCARP Mardan to raise the incomes and welfare of the target population".

The time span selected, the interval between studies, the use of control villages, and the number of researchers, about 30, involved on a long term continuous basis should make the SCARP Mardan evaluation a classic of the genre. Freedman *et al.* (1983) point out their evaluation joins a very small number, citing only three, of like undertakings, and state that they are: "mindful of the burden of laying the groundwork for large scale impact studies of agricultural sector projects in general, for which there are virtually no precedents".

Throughout the duration of the evaluation scheme, the scientific team will monitor its own progress continually. The rationale and the scope of the evaluation will take into account existing approaches, and sound theoretical assumptions will underlie the design of the evaluation project. Throughout the duration of the assessment, as much attention will be given to the intricacies of evaluation as to the evaluation of the project itself.

In the final analysis, the Western and Pakistani group of scholars will continue to build a substantial data bank and develop wide ranging expertise on all aspects of the human-ecological complex in Pakistan. It follows that, given the time span involved, the project should be well on the way towards attaining the characteristics postulated in Model One. It would seem that any one wishing to initiate other similar work in Pakistan would be well advised to consult with the University of Western Ontario Pakistan group of scholars.

Lake Izabal, Guatemala: A Failed Project: the Issues of Poor Planning
and Politics

There is an ongoing dilemma among Canadian academics
committed to Third World affairs, which is the problem of conducting
independent field work abroad, for the continuation of their own
academic training and that of their students, while attempting to be
relevant and useful to host countries. Often such forays abroad are
conducted on low budgets and predicated upon hope rather than long
range planning. In most cases, such work is undertaken
independently of host governments. The results may be worthwhile,
indifferent or disastrous. In the latter case, a lot of energy is
expended, a lot of people are contacted abroad and often
inconvenienced, for nothing; then, as the number of such field
workers, and their rounds of contacts increases, sometimes to rather
frightening proportions, the foreign presence becomes
counterproductive, time wasting for all concerned and, in certain
cases, utterly useless.

One such project, almost a decade ago, involved researchers
from the University of Florida and the University of Western Ontario
in a scheme designed to foster cooperation between Guatemala and
Canada, via exchange of professors and students, with a field training
component for the latter from both countries. The latter component
was seen as being the crucial elements, as there must be mechanisms,
and lots of them, to train young scholars in the art and science of
field work. Consequently, the project was far reaching in scope and
based upon an interdisciplinary approach within the framework of
systems analysis.

The focal point of the project was a Canadian nickel mine site on
Lake Izabal, which had not yet begun to extract mineral. The opening
of the mine, which never did go into substantial production, was to
have had a local, regional, national and international impact. The
University of Florida had already begun base line ecological studies,
as the mine site was being cut out of the forest and developed, and
some anthropological studies had been initiated.

A summary of the research activities that were to have been
conducted at the local, regional, national and international levels is
given in Appendix E. Various specialists were to have conducted
studies along a continuum ranging from the effect of the mine on
nearby agricultural villages to the drainage of funds due to
international flows of profits. In addition, the impact of the mine on
the environment of the lake and adjacent areas was to have been
assessed. For example, if labour were drawn from adjacent villages,
there could be an important impact on forest/agricultural ecology.

Politics intervened during and after the first, and only field season of reconnaissance and planning. The university chosen for twinning in Guatemala had to be politically acceptable to the government in power, which precluded the logical institution that had all the personnel required to make the project effective. Consequently, a different university was chosen, causing serious personnel problems. Moreover, in the field, it became apparent that there were land tenure problems, involving conflict between small farms and large land owners, one of whom was the mine itself. Therefore, field forays at the village level were ill-received in certain political-economic circles.

After the first field season, correspondence, involving Canadian diplomats in Guatemala, suggested a cessation of the project, which under the circumstances was the logical route to follow. The end result was that more than two years of effort, considering the prefield preparation period, were lost.

The conditions under which the Guatemala project began tended towards many of the undesirable elements of Model Two, and continued in that direction during implementation. The research ideas were sound, but the operational and political climate were unfavourable from the start. However, even politically sensitive countries require basic research in the worst way. It is an issue that must be addressed despite the problems and frustrations.

LAND TENURE AND LAND USE: A MAJOR ISSUE

In many countries throughout the Third World, one of the major problems facing researchers in environment and resource management is the matter of land tenure and use. At the macro level, it is a question of agrarian reform, which includes environmental management, that must be addressed. And, at the micro level, there are problems of tenure, occupancy, land use and land abuse.

The problems of agrarian reform have received a lot of attention elsewhere[5] and need not be dwelt upon here. However, some examples from the micro level should serve as a reminder of some of the pressing problems, for resource and environment managers, that are created primarily at the farmstead.

----

[5] The Land Tenure Centre at the University of Wisconsin has a depository that accumulates land and agrarian reform studies from around the world on an ongoing basis.

The first example is from the state of Bihar, India, where the author was involved in assessing the second stage of an irrigation project for an international development agency. During phase one, irrigation had transformed some unfarmable land into a valuable productive agricultural resource. The originally useless land had been donated to the poor by members of an upper cast, at a time when there was no inkling of any impending development scheme. The land had been donated as a grandiose public gesture in response to the pleas of an itinerant holy man, with nobody anticipating the eventual metamorphosis of the land. The true value of the land became evident with irrigation, and the former owners began to fight to reclaim it. They began a campaign of terror against the small farmers, using intimidation, destruction of irrigation works, sabotage of electrical installations and machinery, and even murder. What began as a desirable and viable environmental management project for small farmers became an ugly nightmare, caused by human greed. The issue was land tenure and ownership, and it is one that continues to cause multitudes of problems throughout the Third World.

Another example can be taken from Haiti. As documented by English (1984), and as this author has verified in the field, there are environmental management schemes, including irrigation and reforestation, which have enhanced the agricultural land in some areas. But, as soon as the transformations occurred the land was rapidly and deviously expropriated, passing out of the hands of the small farmers, who had worked it in its poorer state all their lives, into those of absentee landlords, who transformed the previous owners into tenant farmers or wage labourers. Therefore, the projects contributed to the problem of concentrating more wealth in fewer hands which was exactly the opposite of what they were designed to do.

In both the Indian and the Haitian cases, the resource managers were operating under conditions that belong squarely to those listed as the human factors in Model Two. The tragedy in both cases is that the managers had little or no way of knowing what would transpire after their work was completed. It follows that, if possible, land tenure problems should be resolved prior to the initiation of projects, so that the people for whom the projects are designed will in fact be the ultimate beneficiaries.

RESOURCE AND ENVIRONMENTAL ABUSE: A MAJOR ISSUE

The ecology of the Third World is undergoing major abuse by its inhabitants at both macro and micro levels. Examples abound at the latter level as individuals practise deforestation, contribute to soil erosion, contaminate their water supplies and deplete their soil fertility, while carrying out agricultural activities. Offshore, fishermen abuse marine ecosystems using dynamite, illegal seines and traps. They engage in overfishing, capturing undersized specimens, and disregarding advice on conservation and protection of species. At the macro level, there seems to be little or no legislation or concern for the preservation of environment and ecology. Industries such as logging, forestry and mining abuse the ecology with impunity, acting as though responsible ecological and resource management is none of their concern. True, there are examples of corporate responsibility, for instance ALJAM (Alcan Jamaica) has for years rehabilitated mining pits by filling them in, then resodding and reseeding to turn them back into productive pasture land at Kirvine, in Jamaica. Unfortunately, such examples are quite rare in the Third World.

It is obvious that it would be impossible to catalogue the range of environmental and resource abuse at the micro and macro level in the Third World. But, it is not too strong to state that virtually all Third World countries have some ecological problems, and most have poor mechanisms and institutions to deal with them. In fact, because Canadians have perpetrated a great deal of ecological-environmental damage in Canada, for example, in the exploitation of forests, Canada could offer the Third World a great number of experts, who could offer advice on ways to protect environments against damage. But, it would seem that a high priority in ecological-environmental research should be directed at understanding the attitudes of people towards their resources.

The problems are as much socio-economic as ecological. At the micro level, in many cases, the environment is abused as a matter of survival. Whereas at the macro level, decision makers appear to be more concerned with profits than preservation. In the latter case, both Third World and First World people are guilty. Canadians have a great deal of ecological damage to account for in their own country, and they and their Western counterparts seem to have no hesitation to export their capacity for ecological abuse overseas. As individuals, Canadians contribute to all manner of ecological problems in tourist areas. As investors, Canadians can contribute to wide scale environmental damage, which they generally need not worry about, as there are few laws to contend with and if there is legislation to protect the environment, enforcement is seldom very vigorous.

Canada has the experts to carry out sophisticated environmental studies in the Third World. But, in many circumstances, such efforts carried out with little or no reference to the human factor may not be as beneficial as they could be. Problems could develop in those stages where the foreign experts make policy recommendations that involve the participation and/or cooperation of local people.

There is a risk, and it is an issue, that Canadian scientists, many with little or no training or awareness of cultural matters, could be labouring under the false impression that their work approximates Model One. Whereas, in reality, their efforts may be caught in the "vortexes" suggested in Model Two. Therefore, the issue boils down to questions of the organisation of Canadian research capacity in the Third World.

MOBILISING THE EXPERTS: AN ISSUE

In the final analysis, the direction of environmental research in the Third World must be worked out country by country, problem by problem. The basic issue for Canadians is how to be better at the work they have been engaged in for some time. On the one hand, the technical side of the problems continues to receive a great deal of attention, and there are important precedents for field work. For example, one can turn to statements as far back as 1973 by Dasmann *et al.* or to the sectoral guidelines of CIDA (1976) - and the quest goes on and on to do the actual field work in the best possible way. For example, IDRC continues to assess its own work, as shown in the writings of Zandstra *et al.*, (1979). And, IDRC continues to set research priorities all over the world.[6] The Organisation of American States (1969) has developed a methodology for physical resource investigations for economic development which persists as a methodological milestone.

The issue that must be raised does not pertain to the methodology of research, but to the humanity of research. In other words, questions are asked such as: who should carry out the research, under what circumstances, for what length of time, and what would be the best procedural strategies to increase the chances of success?

----

[6] For example, see Daniels and Nestel (1981) for resource allocation in Singapore.

The above questions could be asked with reference to mobilising the required expertise to analyse the current ecological disaster stretching across North Africa. The aggravating fact is that if it were a matter of mobilising resources for war, hundreds of thousands of military people would be thrown line abreast into the battle. But nowhere is there a master plan to mobilise available resources to combat this world disaster of gigantic proportion, nor, indeed, will there ever be. But, we should invoke such global thinking to draw up comprehensive, far reaching and long term plans to tackle the smaller scale problems that Canadians are involved with around the world.

CONCLUSION

It would be interesting to draw up an inventory of all the environmental research and management projects involving Canadians in the Third World, and to attempt to catalogue them in terms of their tendencies to gravitate either towards Model One or Model Two. It is assumed that the results would be placed on a broad continuum.

It is in the interests of all concerned, i.e. of these already in the field, and those that will join them, to devise specific strategies to widen the distance to Model Two and to narrow it to Model One. It would seem that precedents are already in place to accomplish such an aim. It can be argued that the Las Cuevas and SCARP Mardan projects represent a high degree of order in research and management in the one case, and of evaluation, in the other. It would seem logical for all other projects to try and emulate, in one way or another, the excellence of these two.

There should be a particular concern with those projects at the other end of the scale, i.e. those involving short term or brief period commitments, and that might be ill-conceived and/or poorly funded. Some means should be found to decrease such waste of human resources and to channel such researchers into worthwhile, well-conceived projects.

It would be impossible to have one research system, whereby every project and every researcher would go through a centralised screening process. But, some approximation of such a system, i.e. the beginning of closer ties and cooperation between researchers, would be in order. Perhaps, a clearing house, possibly maintained by IDRC, would be a start in the right direction. It would house data on major recognised projects, Canadian and others, and on researchers. It would be designed to allow researchers greater access to each other, and possibly foster more cooperation and coordination, without a lot of bureaucratic red tape.

Certainly, a group of Canadian environmental specialists can draw up research and development priorities for Third World countries. But such an exercise might be more useful if a parallel list could be produced which would link type, location and availability of Canadian and other expertise to each identified problem. In the end, more coordination between all concerned, lead by major funding and research agencies, and more mechanisms to increase the awareness of Canadians called to work overseas, could assist Canadians to assist the Third World.

REFERENCES

Antonini, G. (1981) *Integrated Training and Research Program in Natural Resources Management for the Dominican Republic with Special Applications for Las Cuevas Watershed*, Gainesville, Florida: Center for Latin American Studies.

Canadian International Development Agency (1976) *Sectoral Guides: Rural Development and Renewable Resources*, Ottawa: Canadian International Development Agency (no standard pagination).

Daniels, D. and Nestel, B. (eds.) (1981) *Resource Allocation to Agricultural Research*, Proceedings of a Workshop held in Singapore, June 8-10, Ottawa: International Development Research Centre.

Dasmann, R.F., Milton, J.P. and Freeman, P.H. (1973) *Ecological Principles for Economic Development*, Toronto: John Wiley and Sons, Ltd.

English, E.P. (1984) *Canadian Development Assistance to Haiti*, Ottawa: The North-South Institute.

Espinal, J.J. (1983) "Determination of the level and distribution of household income in the Las Cuevas region of the Dominican Republic: implications for regional development strategies," Gainesville, Florida: University of Florida, unpublished M.Sc. thesis.

Freedman, J. in collaboration with Nickel, W., Loyns, A., Sutherland, V. and Ulrich, M. (1983) *Principles and Design for the Evaluation of a Rural Development Project in Northern Pakistan: SCARP Mardan Evaluation*, Ottawa: Canadian International Development Agency.

Ledesma, H.R. (1983) "Analysis of selected soil properties and environmental relationships in Las Cuevas Watershed, Dominican Republic," Gainesville, Florida: University of Florida, unpublished M.Sc. thesis.

Nova, J.A. (1984) "Optional resource allocation and management in the farming systems of Las Cuevas Watershed Dominican Republic," Gainesville, Florida: University of Florida, unpublished M.Sc. thesis.

Organisation of American States (1969) *Physical Resource Investigations for Economic Development: A Casebook of Organisation of American States Field Experience in Latin America*, Washington: DC: General Secretariat, Organisation of American States.

Posner, J., Antonini, G., Montanez, G., Cecil, R. and Grigsby, M. (1981) "Un Sistema de Clasificaion para las areas de ladera y altiplanos de America Tropical," *Informe tecnico No. 11*, Centro Agronomico Tropical de Investigacion y Ensenanza, Turrialba, Costa Rica, pp. 109-29.

Posner, J., Antonini, G., Montanez, G., Cecil, R. and Grigsby, M. (1983) "Land systems of hill and highland tropical America," *Revista Geografica*, 98 (Julio-Deciembre): 5-22.

Reynoso, F.A. (1983) "Estimation of firewood and charcoal consumption in Las Cuevas Watershed Dominican Republic," Gainesville, Florida: University of Florida, unpublished M.A. thesis.

Zandstra, H., Swanberg, K., Zulberti, C. and Nestel, B. (1979) *CAQUEZA: Living Rural Development*, Ottawa: International Development Research Centre.

APPENDIX A

MODEL ONE

SOME IDEALISED CONDITIONS FOR RESEARCH AND DEVELOPMENT

I

AWARENESS OF THE PHYSICAL UNIVERSE

influence of the geography of neighbouring countries
sets of regions (natural/functional) _____
sets of subareas _____
sets of locations _____

kaleidoscope of scales
basic physical/environmental components (morphology)
basic spatial interaction (physiology)
state and nature of infrastructures/degrees of connectivity
an understanding of the ecosystem

II

AWARENESS OF THE HUMAN CONDITION OF THE RANGE OF HUMAN HETEROGENEITY

function of race, language, religion, education, income, loyalties, politics, health and n number of cultural/social attributes: whose permutations and combinations form n interconnected sets of people, with the sets aggregating and disaggregating
political reality _____ sets of political conditions
economic reality _____ distribution of wealth
social/cultural reality _____ attitudes toward change

III

SOME DESIRABLE CONDITIONS

knowledge of the sets of all projects ____ full cooperation among all project holders in the country
perfect knowledge _____ surfeit of data
competent personnel _____ both local and foreign
sensitised personnel _____ highly motivated
absence of corruption _____ altruism
government support _____ no impediments
best interests of people _____ no ulterior motives
accurate decisions _____ best projects chosen
full understanding of local people _____ and their enthusiastic participation
long term continuity _____ full provision for re-inforcers

IV

THRUST TOWARDS PROPER POLICIES

sensitivity towards priorities _____ local as well as national
desirablity of long term pre-project assessment
ongoing evaluation of project
long term post project assessment

ability to pre-judge impact on people and their environment

V

WILLINGNESS TO CONTINUE TO LEARN

the universe of ideas, conditions and variables not expressed in I to
IV above

APPENDIX B

MODEL TWO

*SOME MAJOR IMPEDIMENTS TO ACCURATE RESEARCH AND
PROPER DEVELOPMENT*

I

ENVIRONMENTAL DAMAGE/ABUSE

AGENTS: nationals, expatriates, either private or public projects.
SCALE: on a continuum from the farmstead to huge regions.
SEVERE PROBLEMS: depletion of fish stocks, ruination of coastal
    environments, deforestation, soil erosion, siltation, damages
    resulting from river modifications, ecological damage caused by
    mining and the development of major infrastructures, and air and
    water pollution.

II

IMPEDIMENTS CAUSED BY PEOPLE

HUMAN HETEROGENEITY: dividing people into different groups
    with different interests, often antagonistic.
CONFRONTATIONS: between groups, either directly through
    violence or indirectly through manipulation.
POLITICAL REALITY: interference, coercion, repression and
    oppression.
ECONOMIC REALITY: unequal distribution of wealth, unequal
    access to resources and massive poverty.

SOCIAL-CULTURAL REALITY: resistance to change, criminal acts, distrust, fear, pragmatism, deviousness, and other such attributes.

III

DETRIMENTAL CONDITIONS

overall lack of knowledge _____ implementation without proper data

incompetent personnel _____ both foreign and national

insensitive personnel _____ poorly motivated

corruption and graft _____ pragmatism

government resistance _____ impediments

interests of people not considered _____ ulterior motives

poor decisions _____ improper choice of projects

misunderstanding of local people _____ resistance to change

short term commitment _____ no training of personnel to re-inforce project

selfishness _____ no cooperation between different groups doing different projects

cultural clashes _____ misunderstanding between locals and foreigners

bureaucratic impediments _____ monumental waste of time

IV

DISTORTED POLICIES

insensitivity towards priorities _____ local and national

lack of project assessment _____ prior to, during and after the fact

inability to pre-judge impact on people

V

OTHER CONSIDERATIONS

sets of unknown factors that may doom a project before it sees the light of day

APPENDIX C

*RESEARCH AND DEVELOPMENT IN THE MANAGEMENT OF
THE LAS CUEVAS WATERSHED*

I

SYSTEMS ANALYSIS

OPERATIONAL: modelling and computer simulation; planning watershed development and protection; resources management, conservation, erosion control, water management.
MAJOR SUBSYSTEMS: silviculture, forest productivity, resource management zoning, hydrological monitoring/sedimentation, land and farming, socio-economic.
MAJOR VARIABLE GROUPS: soils, natural subregions, slopes bioclimates, actual land use and tenure.

II

SPECIAL TARGETS FOR ACTION

RESOURCE MANAGEMENT: erosion control, farm production, new technologies, provision of land titles.
RURAL WELFARE: promotion of group dynamics and actions; and building institutional services for health, schooling and nutrition.
DEVELOPMENT: improvement of marketing system, fostering rural industries, building on the skills found in small towns.
SOILS: determination of soil productivity and evaluation of erosion potential, evaluation of sedimentation potential, determination of water availability for crop growth, and climatic variations and the probability of hurricane damage.
LAND: land use evaluation, determination of potential land use
SPECIFIC RESOURCES: Farms and their management, cropping patterns, forestry management.
RURAL WELFARE: population growth, rural to urban migration, social changes, community organisation, communication, education, health, nutrition, rural forestry, transportation, markets.

APPENDIX D

SCARP MARDAN PROJECT PAKISTAN[1]

I

MAJOR WORKS

IRRIGATION: remodelling a system of 50,000 hectares increasing channel capacities.
TILE DRAINAGE: installing about 29,000 hectares.
SURFACE DRAINAGE: Remodelling about 40,800 hectares.
LAND LEVELLING: about 8,100 hectares.
RECLAIMING: About 5,700 hectares of abandoned or marginally productive saline-alkaline lands.
AGRICULTURAL EXTENSION SYSTEM: introducing   and implementing such a system.
TECHNICAL ASSISTANCE: for preparation for civil works, for implementing agricultural extension and to prepare other irrigation/drainage projects.

II

LIMITED EXAMPLES
A FEW OF THE DIMENSIONS OF THE EVALUATIONS

OBJECTIVE: assess the sociological/economic impact of the project at the very early stages, and again at its completion.
SCOPE: very broad; e.g. changing household composition, changing income levels of respondent households, changes in farm practices.
SAMPLE: a large stratified sample of villages and households.
ECONOMIC INFLUENCES: e.g. price variation, farm size, yields and incomes.
NON-PROJECT RELATED FACTORS: In order to distinguish changes due to project-related and to non-project-related factors.
FARM ECONOMY: e.g. cropping patterns, resource use, marketing of farm inputs and outputs, employment patterns, distribution of wealth.

----

[1] From Freedman *et al.* (1983) including the quotes.

SOCIAL RELATIONS: e.g. those among households at the village
level which have occurred in the course of project
implementation.

APPROACH: many are reviewed, a systems approach is used; then,
the answers sought are in the WHY category, not just the
WHAT.

NOTE: "The project environment is presumed to influence the inputs
as much as the inputs influence the environment."

PRINCIPAL GOAL: "Is to describe, free of judgements about the
worth of the project and its effects, the changes in the Mardan
area socio-economy, attributable to the implementation of
SCARP Mardan."

KEY VARIABLES: sets of variables related to all the above broken
down to individual elements and monitored over long periods of
time. Indicators and data gathering strategies have been worked
out.

APPENDIX E

THE LAKE IZABAL SYSTEMS' STUDY
A PARTIAL LIST OF VARIABLES

I

THE SETTING

LOCAL: the mine site at El Estor.

AREAL: the effect of the mine on the Lake Izabal area.

REGIONAL: the mine as a focal point of the Lake Izabal-Rio Dulce
ecosystem.

NATIONAL: the mine as an economic growth pole and an economic
multiplier.

INTERNATIONAL: the international nickel mining system; flows of
capital (inputs/outputs), international monetary and market
forces, international politics and decision making.

II

THE RESEARCH ISSUES

LOCAL: the impact of the mine on the adjacent land and marine ecosystems, the impact on human ecology.

AREAL: the capacity of the mine to modify socio-economic conditions in and around the Lake Izabal-Rio Dulce System.

REGIONAL: the changing economic base, the modification of agricultural systems, the impact on demographic structures, the changing labour base, modernisation and the impact of technology, immigration of urbanites into the area, the changing commercial base, changing family structure due to the arrival of wage labour, the changing economic input-output factors into the region, the regional multiplier effect.

NATIONAL: the impact on national GNP, the growth pole effect, the planning and construction of infrastructures, the reinvestment of profits, the hidden economic factors.

INTERNATIONAL: the matter of the manipulation of nickel supplies, and labour forces, in the global nickel mining system.

III

POLITICAL PROBLEMS

WARFARE: guerilla activities, in urban and rural areas, government military operations.

INTELLECTUAL GROUPS: political activities of university faculty and students, polarised politics, bloody animosity culminating in assassination, repression, oppression and death. Anti-intellectual policies.

LAND TENURE: land tenure problems, coercion, land seizure, and peasant repression.

TRADITIONAL FOODS: long-standing blood feuds between different political fractions and individuals. Left and right dichotomy in the country, death squads.

ECONOMIC ROOTS: fear of activism if ecological-impact studies encounter environmental-resource abuse. Policies of interference with objective studies.

CHAPTER 3

RESEARCH PRIORITIES FOR PLANNING WATER RESOURCE
DEVELOPMENT

Nalni D. Jayal
Institute for Ecology Research and
Environment Management
New Delhi, India

INTRODUCTION

Planning for Water Resource Development in Third World
countries like India has first to take note of the destruction of water
resources through the invisible ecological impact of economic
activities. Arresting destruction is a precondition for development.
Research priorities for water resource development must therefore
include research into processes by which the renewability and
sustained availability of water is being undermined, as well as research
into processes by which water resources can be stabilised and
augmented. Conservation of water resources through the maintenance
of the essential ecological processes which replenish and renew water
for plant, animal and human life is the first critical step in the
planning of water projects (Jayal, 1984). Without ensuring
conservation, water availability will decrease in spite of an increase in
water projects. This, in fact, has been the history of water
development projects in the past. The decrease in availability of
water in spite of increase in investment in water projects arises, in my
view, from three biases in resource use - the temperate bias, the
departmental bias, and the engineering bias. The temperate bias is
the extension of knowledge of temperate ecosystems to the

management of tropical ecosystems. The departmental bias is the tendency to see a resource system, not as an ecologically interlinked integral whole, but as a fragmented bundle of unrelated and isolated resources to be managed by fragmented departments. The engineering bias is an approach to problems and solutions that is related to the departmental bias and offers engineering solutions to resource problems which are ecological in nature and which have to be responded to ecologically. These biases guide Third World development into directions which are resource destructive and hence unsustainable. Research for Third World development in general, and for water resource development in particular, needs to unravel these biases and to transcend them in order to generate knowledge about resources, which is ecologically more appropriate and authentic in Third World contexts.

THE TEMPERATE BIAS

Tropical and Temperate Zones

     The Third World is largely located in the tropical zone. The Third World as a tropical world is different from the temperate world in which the industrialised countries of the North are located. The contemporary location of poverty in the tropics and affluence in the temperate zones has less to do with the resource endowment of these regions and is more closely related to the resource exploitation and resource mismanagement of the tropical world. The dominance of the Third World by some countries in the North in the process of colonisation initiated a process by which scientists and experts from the temperate zone began applying their limited knowledge to a very different ecological context. Scientists from England brought sylvicultural, agricultural, hydrological development models from their own environments and applied them uncritically to the tropical world. Land use in the Western Ghats and the Himalaya which receive rainfall of about 3,000 mm within a short span of three months was based on knowledge generated in London which would receive the equivalent precipitation over 25 years. Sylvicultural systems of temperate zone forest management were applied to tropical forests, undermining the potential of sustained yields of biomass and introducing severe hazards of soil erosion and twin problems of floods and drought. This temperate bias in resource use in the tropical

world has generated serious ecological problems related to water
resource conservation and development.

Water Management in the Tropics

The management of conserving water resources is not as severe -
in temperate zones. In fact, presumptions of water management are
often diametrically opposite under temperate conditions. Hibbert
(1967) reported that results from 30 studies indicated that, in general,
reduction in forest cover increased water yield or reforestation was
accompanied by decreased water yield. Clear-cutting lodgepole pine
in Colorado increased stream flow about 30 per cent (Wilm and
Dunfond, 1948) and removal of all woody vegetation from a watershed
in Coweeta, North Carolina, increased stream flow more than 70 per
cent the first year. Over the whole United States, about one-fourth of
the total precipitation escapes as stream flow and three-fourths is
returned to the atmosphere by evapotranspiration (Ackerman and Lof
1959). In India, 48 per cent of the precipitation is consumed through
evaporation and transpiration. The remaining 52 per cent of this
precipitation constitutes the nation's average annual national runoff.
It is this resource that provides the needs of agriculture, industry and
domestic requirements (Chaturvedi, 1974).

In India, the impact of clearfelling would quite clearly not be
increased water yields, but increased floods in the monsoon and
increased water scarcity in the dry period. Thus, as a consequence of
the mismanagement of catchments, the flood prone areas had doubled
by 1980 to 40 million hectares from 20 million hectares in 1971, and
the constantly expanding drought prone areas now cover 59 million
hectares. To cite an example, the immediate impact of clearfelling
the natural forests in the Dhaola subcatchment of the Neora Valley of
the Darjeeling Himalaya by the West Bengal Forest Development
Corporation a few years ago was to dry up almost completely a
valuable source of perennial water sought to augment the very scarce
drinking water supply in that region - a problem itself created by
deforestation over the past few decades in hills renowned for their
splendid forests. There are a number of reasons why vegetation has
different impacts on water availability under temperate and tropical
conditions. The seasonality of rainfall implies that runoff and
infiltration is critical to water availability. The infiltration-percolation
path of the hydrological cycle is crucial to water yields under tropical
conditions. Under conditions of uniformly distributed rainfall, the
uniform availability of water is ensured even if the infiltration pathway

is bypassed. When precipitation is incident as snow, infiltration on gentle relief is ensured by snow melt and is temporarily separated from incidence of precipitation.

The natural vegetation of the tropics, both in humid, as well as arid regions, is best adapted to water management under local conditions. Changes induced in the vegetation through the temperate zone bias produces serious problems for water management in the tropics. For instance, the root system of indigenous species is normally adapted to the groundwater level and a change in the root zone of introduced species will result in a change in the capillary rise, soil moisture storage, groundwater storage, and base flow formation. Similarly, a decrease of interception by introducing plants with reduced leaf areas leads to an increase in surface runoff and erosion under intensive tropical rainfall. The large scale introduction of eucalyptus throughout India, and the expansion of pine in the Himalaya under forest management with a temperate zone bias has been insensitive to the role of vegetation in managing seasonal rainfall to make water available throughout the year, either as base flow in streams or as soil moisture.

Indigenous Systems of Water Management

The temperate bias in knowledge related to water resources has a second implication. It tends to ignore the indigenous knowledge of the tropical world. "Scientific forestry" is equated with the replacement of ecologically sound tropical systems of forest management by temperate zone systems. "Scientific agriculture" is similarly the replacement of sustainable and productive tropical farming systems with ecologically inappropriate models imported from temperate zones. All cultures have, however, had ecologically, and scientifically, sound systems of knowledge about resources. Since regions are ecologically diverse - these knowledge systems have been pluralistic. The false assumption that everything scientific is universal has rejected these systems of knowledge as unscientific and has led to the universalisation of knowledge peculiar to temperate contexts or created in temperate contexts. Large dams have been one of these universalisations. Large water projects have often destroyed more efficient water projects used traditionally for centuries. In the Mexican region of Oaxaca, different ecological conditions within a short distance of each other led to entirely different systems of water transportation (Kirkby, 1977). In Madras Presidency in South India at one time, irrigation by small tanks and canals, which the villagers managed themselves, irrigated collectively an area equal to that irrigated by all the larger works which have been constructed by the British Government in that Presidency.

In the Mysore region, a highly developed tank system of irrigation has existed from ancient times. This system consisted of a single series of several hundred and in some cases, over a thousand reservoirs linked together and forming such continued chains of works that not a single drop of water falling in the catchment is lost in seasons of drought, and but little in ordinary seasons.

Water resources research for Third World development needs to take more seriously the scientific and ecological value of indigenous knowledge and technology and it needs to be more cautious while extrapolating knowledge from temperate zones to the tropical world. Transcending the temperate bias is an important element of research on Third World resources and environment.

THE DEPARTMENTAL BIAS

Related to the temperate bias is the departmental bias in the research and design of many water projects. The holistic knowledge of integrated ecosystems has in the past given way to fragmented compartmentalised knowledge on individual resources. Forests are viewed as timber deposits, forestry is taught in forest departments and managed by forest departments. The impact of forestry practices on soil and water regimes is not a central part of forestry management. Nor do managers of water projects see their work as related to the nature of vegetation in the ecosystem. This departmental bias has contributed to the water crisis and will need to be overcome through integrated approaches to research and development related to water resources. This approach would remain incomplete in the absence of people's participation in the planning and management of water projects, since water is a transient resource interacting with soil and vegetation systems.

The Soil-Vegetation-Water System

The water resource crisis is no longer a futuristic crisis for India. It appears to be the most severe crisis receiving the scantiest attention, both at the level of scientific expertise as well as at the level of policy, planning and management. The water crisis has to be viewed as arising from the total disruption of the hydrological cycle the set of related ecological processes by which water is made available to an ecosystem through precipitation, runoff, infiltration, soil water moisturisation, groundwater recharge, and finally returned to the atmosphere.

Destabilisation of the hydrological cycle implies that changes are introduced in the relative proportions between rapid flood waters and delayed groundwater based runoff forming the dependable river flow. Such destabilisation is the result of manipulations of the land surface involving major modifications of the soil-vegetation system. Modifications in the soil-vegetation system are reflected in changes both in the yield and seasonality of water availability. Because soil and vegetation systems are so intrinsically linked to one another, the water crisis is an aspect of the ecological crisis which is also leading to the erosion of soil and the erosion of biological productivity. It is useful to approach the analysis of this crisis from the perspective of water resources because water is a transient and dynamic factor and because it is central to the survival of plant, animal and human life (Widstrand, 1980).

The failure to relate modifications in land use with water resource dynamics has led to vast and serious problems of floods, soil erosion, land aridisation, waterlogging and salinisation. This paper focuses on the relationship between the soil-vegetation-water system and the implications of changes in these relationships for water resource availability. It stresses the extremely important but often neglected interdependence between soil conservation, conservation of biota and water conservation since soil cover and vegetation are key factors in the runoff formation process and in the renewal and recharge of water storages.

Maharashtra's Water Crisis

Maharashtra State provides a dramatic illustration of how the changes in land use are linked with water use. Ninety-three per cent of Maharashtra State is occupied by hard rocks consisting of the Deccan Trap. In the Deccan Trap the storage space for groundwater is developed because of secondary features like joints, weathering, fissuring, etc. All these features do not occur in uniform fashion both in depth and in lateral extent. This results in the fact that reservoir space gets delineated by irregular boundaries both vertically and laterally forming disconnected or feebly connected groundwater pools/pockets/minibasins (Jaglab, 1984; Maggerwar, 1984). In the Deccan Trap, therefore, there is nothing like a subsoil water table.

Water is stored in joints and bedding planes and is recharged locally. Energisation of pumps has mushroomed after the 1972 drought when financial assistance created heavy subsidies for mechanised withdrawals of water. This led to overexploitation of groundwater. The Groundwater Survey and Development Agency of Maharashtra has found that out of 1,481 watersheds in the State, there is overexploitation of 77 watersheds spread over 14 districts.

The problem is extremely acute in the five districts of Ahamdnagar, Sangli, Jalgaon, Dhule and Nasik. Abuse of water for water-intensive cultivation has created a severe drinking water crisis and a severe food crisis. As the Chief Minister of Maharashtra stated at the last National Development Council meeting, in the Sixth Plan 17,112 villages were identified as facing drinking water problems of which 15,302 villages are likely to be covered by the end of 1985, leaving 1,810 villages to be covered in the ensuing Seventh Five Year Plan. The rapid depletion of groundwater resources has, however, increased the problem of villages with no source of drinking water to a staggering 23,000 villages.

Sugarcane cultivation is among the cash crops which has an extremely high water demand. In the area around one sugar factory alone, sugarcane cultivation with groundwater irrigation has increased dramatically over two decades.

	Area Under Sugarcane (well irrigated) (Hectares)
1961-62	3248
1971-72	6990
1981-82	17612

Incomes have risen as a result of shifting from rainfed, coarse grain production to an irrigated cash crop. But the costs have been heavy. Manerajree village of Tasgaon Taluk is among those that have benefitted financially but lost materially by the expansion of energised groundwater withdrawal for sugarcane cultivation. A new water scheme with a potential supply of 50,000 litres was commissioned in November 1981 at a cost of Rs.693,000. The source well yield lasted for one year and it went dry by November 1982. For increasing yields, three bores were taken near the well for 60 metres. The yield from all the three with power pumps was 50,000 litre/day for 1982 and all bores had gone dry by November 1983. There has been continuous tanker service since 1983. In 1984, one bore of 60 metres depth was taken which had water but also went dry. At present, water is being brought by tanker from 15 kms distance. More than 2,000 privately owned wells in this sugarcane country have also gone dry.

Drought and Desertification

There is a tendency to associate rainfall failure with the water famine and to see the lack of rain as the cause for the disappearance of water. Yet, rainfall failure cannot lead to disappearance of groundwater by itself because groundwater storages are the cumulative effect of long periods of percolation and recharge. For instance, the deep aquifers under the Sahara are recharged at the rate of 4 km^3 per year and their total capacity is 15,000 km^3 per year. This means that it would take nearly 4,000 years at the present rate of recharge to fill these formations. Quite clearly, groundwater will not get exhausted merely because rains fail during one year. On the other hand, even with regular rainfall, groundwater depletion can take place if withdrawals exceed annual recharge. Traditional cropping patterns in arid zones have been based on effective use of soil moisture recharged by rainfall, with irrigation used as a protective measure. High yielding varieties have high groundwater demand, and this is not matched with water availability. At the national level, current patterns of agricultural development will outstrip water availability before the turn of the century. 1980-1990 is a drinking decade and one thing that must be ensured during this period is that water is not abused by some so that vital needs for drinking water are denied the poorer, less privileged groups. This case of privatisation of a common resource needs to be strictly under social control. Much more serious research is needed on assessments of recharge rates to control withdrawal of groundwater. Research is also needed at the micro-level under field conditions to determine crop-water relationships to select appropriate cropping patterns.

Water scarcities which render plant, animal and human life impossible in a certain environment are not a new problem. Such conditions where scarcity of water puts limits on survival are what desertification is all about. Desertification has a thousand year old history with the decay of the North African granary of Imperial Rome, and the Middle East. It is often assumed that desertification spreads from a desert core. While some climatic deserts such as the Sahara are being desertified on their borders, the much more common condition is the creation of desertified land from any climatic desert. There are no natural deserts in the Great Plains, but desertification has occurred there. There are no natural deserts in the Deccan Plateau, but land use is evolving in such a way that a serious threat of desertification exists. Desertification is a man-made problem. Drought aggravates the condition, but is not the cause.

THE ENGINEERING BIAS

Ecological and Engineering Approaches to Water Development

"Engineers enjoy the challenge of designing irrigation schemes, particularly when they are in large scale, and therefore speak of water 'wasted' when it runs into the sea" (Clark, 1970). This engineering bias fails to see the natural river flows as critical to drainage, to recharge of groundwater, and to the maintenance of the balance between fresh water and saline water in the coastal regions. The engineering bias in water use generates large projects which create serious social and ecological instabilities.

The impounding of water in large dams leads to deforestation in the catchment which changes the micro-climate and leads to soil erosion, thus decreasing the availability of water. The transport of large volumes of water over large distances wastes water in seepage. The introduction of large volumes of water beyond the natural drainage capacity of the ecosystem disrupts the hydrological cycle and results in waterlogging and salinity.

During the past three decades, India has spent over Rs.100 billion on developing irrigation facilities, and by the end of this year (1985), the total area covered by irrigation will be 40 mha. Moreover, 6 mha of arable land has become unproductive through waterlogging and another 7 mha has been similarly affected by salinity.

The Kabini project is a good case study of a water development project which became the cause of the disruption of the hydrological cycle in the basin. The Kabini project has a submersion area of 6,000 acres, but it led to the clearfelling of 30,000 acres of primeval forests in the catchments to rehabilitate displaced villages. As a consequence local rainfall fell from 60 inches to 45 inches, and high siltation rates have already drastically reduced the life of the project. Large areas of well developed coconut gardens and paddy fields have been laid waste through waterlogging and salinity within two years of irrigation from the project. The story of the Kabini project is a classic case of how the water crisis is being created by the very projects aimed at increasing water availability or stabilising water flows.

River valley projects are considered the usual solution to meeting the water needs of agriculture, or for controlling floods or mitigating droughts. More than 1,554 large dams have been built in India during the past three decades. It is estimated that about 79 mha-metres of water can be used annually from the surface flow in Indian rivers but less than 25 mha-metres is actually utilised. The obvious answer so far has been to provide storage capacity in large reservoirs behind huge and costly dams. Between 1951 and 1980, India has spent Rs.75,100 million on major or medium irrigation dams. Yet the return from this large investment has been far less than anticipated. In fact, where irrigated lands should yield at least 5 tonnes of grain per ha in India, it has remained at 1.7 tonnes per ha. The annual losses from irrigation projects caused by unexpectedly low water availability, heavy siltation reducing storage capacity, waterlogging, etc. now amount to Rs.4,270 million.

These large river valley projects, on the one hand, cause deforestation in catchments, and on the other hand, cause waterlogging in the command area. The option created for water use is, therefore, unsustainable. Nonsustainability is also built into the ecological impact of large irrigation works on cropping patterns. Large discharges demand uniformity, uniformity in discharge compels uniformity in cropping patterns which decreases genetic diversity and increases vulnerability to pests. Trees on farms are cut in the command area for land development, thus further destabilising soil moisture and disrupting the soil nutrient cycle and destroying the habitat of pest-predators.

Old irrigation systems have lasted for centuries because they were based on prudent use of water which saves catchments and prevents waterlogging. The impounding was done by a series of small dams, or tanks. The distribution channels were lined with farm trees performing the dual function of preventing seepage and providing agricultural inputs in terms of fertiliser or fodder which, in turn, improve soil structure and prevent waterlogging or salinity.

The engineering interventions for water conservation have failed to view the central role of humus forming trees as the most powerful means for water conservation in vulnerable catchments and in fragile tropical agricultural ecosystems. The integrity of the soil-vegetation-water system is crucial to water conservation, both in forests and on farmlands. Water conservation strategies are, therefore, ultimately related to strategies for soil conservation and the conservation of genetic diversity in forests and croplands. There is an urgent need to shift from engineering interventions to ecological interventions. Ecological interventions in the tropics take into account the uniqueness and variability in the structure, function and dynamics of tropical ecosystems. Ecological approaches aim at increasing productivity while minimising resource use and resource wastage.

Desertification and Role of Soil as Water Reservoir

While water is recognised as a central input in plant productivity, there is generally a failure in recognising that the soil is a massive water reservoir and that the capacity of this reservoir is dependent on the vegetative cover as well as the soil structure which determines the water retentivity of soil (Kovda, 1980; Teare and Peat, 1983; United Nations, 1977). In arid zones where vegetative growth, both in forests, as well as farms, is entirely dependent on recharge of soil moisture by rain, an extremely important, and the only viable and sustaining mechanism for water conservation, is the addition of organic matter. Organic matter or humus enhances the water retentivity of soils dramatically. This mechanism of conserving water as soil moisture assumes critical importance in the tropics where rainfall is seasonal and has to be effectively stored in the soil to support plant growth in the arid periods. Conserving soil moisture is an insurance against desertification in arid climates. Adding organic matter increases soil moisture in situ and contributes dramatically to increased food production.

Besides the technology of water conservation in soil through organic matter, intercropping is another technology for avoiding crop failure in rainfed farming. Evidence exists that sole-cropped sorghum fails once in eight years and pigeonpea, once in five years, but that a sorghum-pigeonpea intercrop fails only once in 36 years (Kanwar, 1981). Drought and desertification are two different ecological phenomena. Drought is an extended dry period. Under conditions of seasonal rainfall, plants and soils have to constantly cope with drought. Drought gets transformed into desertification when the moisture retentivity of soils goes down due to decline in organic matter input to the soil or due to excessive uptake by vegetation modifications which involve the introduction of the new plant species into a particular ecozone. Organic matter input declines because of decline in farm animals and decline in farm trees which are the primary producers of organic fertilisers for soils on farmlands. In forest areas, organic matter return suffers through deforestation which reduces humus formation through litter return. Sometimes inappropriate afforestation strategies can become the source of depletion of soil moisture and land aridisation. The large scale introduction of eucalyptus hybrid in India is contributing to such land aridisation first by its high water uptake and second by its insignificant contribution to humus formation. There is no scientific work done yet on the water relations of indigenous tree species but it is apparent that their root systems, their crown morphology, their physiology are adapted to the hydrological conditions prevailing in the tropics and that indigenous or naturalised plant species contribute to water conservation in a number of ways.

GAPS IN SCIENTIFIC KNOWLEDGE FOR CONSERVATION AND DEVELOPMENT OF WATER RESOURCES IN THE THIRD WORLD

The knowledge base for resource use for development has been limited by the temperate zone bias, the departmental bias and the engineering bias. Large gaps exist in research for development of tropical countries.

An important area of investigation is the relationship between quality of life and resource stability on the one hand, and the quality of life and the cash nexus on the other. Too often assumptions of backwardness have been made without an authentic evaluation of the quality of life.

Ecological approaches to water conservation and development need to be scientifically compared for cost-effectiveness with the capital-intensive engineering models which have been the dominant paradigm.

Serious existing gaps in knowledge on the interaction between plants, soils and water in tropical ecosystems and the interplay with groundwater need to be studied to optimise water use in forestry and agriculture, as the role of soil and water for plant production in tropical systems is of critical importance for improving food production and promoting economic development.

Scientific and systems studies for assessing the ecological and economical cost-benefits by major water impoundments and irrigation systems need to be carried out to determine whether such costly investments should be made in future or alternative strategies adopted for a more natural approach towards increasing productivity of agriculture.

REFERENCES

Ackerman, E.A. and Lof, G.O.G. (1959) *Technology in American Water Development*, Baltimore, Maryland: John Hopkins Press.

Clark, C. (1970) *The Economics of Irrigation*, Oxford: Pergamon Press.

Chaturvedi, M.C. (1974) *Water in Second India*, Second India Series Ford Foundation.

Economic Times (1984) "Rising saline groundwater in Haryana, Rs.800.00 cr. plan mooted to eradicate menace," October 31.

Hebalkar, V.B. (1984) *Irrigation by groundwater in Maharashtra*, Government of Maharashtra: Directorate of Ground Water Surveys and Development Agency.

Hibbert, A.R. (1967) "Forest treatment effects on water yield," in Sopper, W.E. and Lull, H.W. (eds.), *Forest Hydrology*, Oxford: Pergamon Press, pp. 527-43.

ICRISAT (1981) *Improving the Management of India's Deep Black Soils*.

Jaglab, P.N. (1984) *Planning groundwater exploration in Deccan Trap*," Government of Maharashtra: Directorate of Ground Water Surveys and Development Agency.

Jayal, N.D. (1984) *Destruction of Water Resources*, IUCN GA, Madrid.

Kanwar, J.S. (1981) "Rain water management: the key to increased agricultural production in deep black soils," ICRISAT.

Kirkby, A. (1977) *Primitive Irrigation in Geographical Hydrology*, in Chooley, R.J. (ed.), Methuen.

Kovda, V.A. (1980) *Land Aridisation and Drought Control*, Boulder, Colorado: West View.

Maggerwar, C.H. (1984) *Techno-Economic Feasibility of Groundwater Development for Irrigation Through Dugwells, Tubewells and Borewells*, Government of Maharashtra: Directorate of Ground Water Surveys and Development Agency.

Sharma, Sudhindra (1984) *The High Cost of Irrigation*, Indian Express, November 4.

Teare, I.D. and Peat, M.M. (1983) *Crop-Water Relations*, New York: John Wiley.

United Nations (1977) *Desertification: Its Causes and Consequences*, Oxford: Pergamon Press.

Widstrand, C. (ed.) (1980) *Water Conflicts and Research Priorities*, Oxford: Pergamon Press.

Wilm, H.G. and Dunfond, E.G. (1948) *Effect of Timber Cutting on Water available for Stream Flow from a Lodgepole Pine Forest*, Washington, D.C.: U.S. Department Agricultural Technical Bulletin, No. 968.

CHAPTER 4

LOCAL RESOURCES FOR A HUMAN ENVIRONMENT

Raúl Vicencio
Cooperative Programs Division
International Development Research Centre
Ottawa, Ontario

INTRODUCTION

In the same manner that government agencies, ministries or states must make decisions on the allocation of their economic resources to different possible avenues of economic and social advancement, development aid organisations, such as IDRC, try to arrive at rational policies to guide their support of those efforts. In what follows, some alternatives for the utilisation of natural resources will be presented and the case will be argued for a policy of concentrating in the development of those resources for which there are existing or potential local sources and markets.

Resource and effort allocation for economic development is a classic problem of decision under uncertainty: it is possible under certain conditions to estimate the benefits that may accrue to the economy from certain levels of investment and effort in a given, well known and narrow sector. However, the decision on whether to concentrate on one sector versus another, or more realistically, on what mix of investment in different sectors of the economy one should strive for, remains largely indeterminable, a reflection of what kind of society the planners hope for rather than what has the best chance of success.

For most of the developing world, a significant part of their economic history has been conditioned by the exploitation of their natural resources to supply the needs of metropolitan centres in the developed world: the colonial powers in the past, nowadays the trading nations of the industrialised world or the richer Third World countries. This has meant that resource-exporting countries experience not only distortions in their overall economies but also that their social and cultural life is strongly influenced by decisions made elsewhere and for purposes alien to their own society.

The economic life of Ghana, for example, has been altered drastically by the Volta River Project (Hart, 1980), although not in the way originally envisaged: after 25 years, the main users of the hydroelectricity produced are the aluminium refineries. Due to the expectation of abundant and cheap electricity created by the building of the dam, smaller generators were shipped to northern Ghana. In recent years, when hydropower production slumped due to the drought, electricity was assigned to aluminium refineries on a priority basis and the city of Accra and surrounding area, with little or no emergency power supply, suffered worse power outages than it did before the dam was built. Other examples abound.

NATURAL RESOURCES AND THE ENVIRONMENT AT IDRC

All of the five IDRC divisions support research programs that deal with natural resources and environmental issues. In addition, a Centre-wide Energy Fund provides support for energy-related projects.

- The Agriculture, Food and Nutrition Sciences Division supports research in the areas of soil conservation and irrigation.
- The Social Sciences Division deals with economic and social aspects of natural resources exploitation and trade.
- The Health Sciences Division funds research in water supply-sanitation and in occupational health/environmental toxicology.
- The Information Sciences Division finances the setting up of information systems related to natural resources/environment and supports remote sensing systems.
- The Cooperative Programs Division, which supports research collaboration between Third World and Canadian researchers, has the largest share of activities in this field. Through its Earth Sciences program, it funds, among other areas, projects in hydrology and hydrogeology and in environmental geology;

in mineral resources investigations, primarily industrial minerals, agrominerals and building materials; in small-scale mining and minesite metallurgy; in geotechnical engineering and in the application of selected geophysical methods to problems of natural resources and the environment.

The rationale for selecting these areas for support is a simple one: it is one of trying to maximise the chances that the results of research will benefit directly the poorest sectors of society in developing countries. It is also a rationale common to other programs throughout the Centre. IDRC tries to direct its efforts as much as possible to the primary user of the products of research while fulfilling its mandate to support applied research "relevant to the needs of the developing countries".

Another reason why the earth sciences (broadly understood) have been selected as an important area of support in the context of Cooperative Programs activities: it is an area of considerable Canadian expertise that has contributed significantly to the economic development of this country. Canadian prospectors and their modern counterparts, geologists and geophysicists, for example, have played an important role in the creation of wealth from natural resources. The Geological Survey of Canada is well known around the world as an example of a progressive, highly competent institution in its field.

But there is one more and very important reason why the Canadian experience, and that of Ontario in particular, is very relevant to the problems of developing countries in the field of the use of natural resources and of their consequences. Alone among the industrial nations, Canada derives most of its foreign trade income and a significant fraction of its total economic output from the exploitation and sale of its natural resources. Not only has this been an important factor in the country's economic development, but some have seen in it as well an overall formative element in the fabric of the nation.

In any case, the analogy to the situation of resource-exploiting developing countries has been pointed out on many occasions and need not be repeated here. What is important is that this experience both sensitises Canadians to the issue of overdependence on natural resource exploitation for exports and enables some of them to see more clearly similar issues in developing countries. We could then propose approaches to solutions based on the Canadian experience, help Third World countries to increase the labour content of their exports, and to concentrate more on providing goods and services for the local population, therefore helping to make the transition to a more balanced economy.

RESEARCH COLLABORATION AND THE ROLE OF CANADIAN RESEARCH INSTITUTIONS

Participants in this conference will be exposed to brief accounts of a couple of IDRC-funded collaborative research projects in developing countries. There is no set pattern for the kind of cooperation we envisage, but some comments may help you see, on the basis of experience so far, what kind of approach is more likely to produce successful results.

First, IDRC is an agency that responds to research needs perceived and articulated in developing countries. The setting up of a cooperative research project works best when the need and will to act on the part of the Third World partner can be matched with the research capability of the Canadians in a spirit of common understanding of research needs, expectationss and ways of operating. We would like a partnership of peers.

Second, the matter of research priorities in the Third World has to be considered. Naturally, in the case of development of natural resources, this is a very country-specific matter, and one in which the available options may be limited. Bolivian and Chilean planners are quite aware of their countries overdependence on tin and copper mining respectively, but in the short term, a considerable improvement on their balance of payments (and therefore alleviation of their large foreign debt) could be affected by judicious applied research in mining and metallurgy. In the medium and long term however, serious consideration must be given to developing those resources that are more likely to result in improved standards of living for the local population and that at the same time present a smaller risk of having the local economy depend on events beyond the control of the people affected by those events.

In the case of environmental problems the situation is a bit better from the point of view of planning, but there seems to be little contact between planning and reality, as is the case in many industrial countries as well. Until fairly recent times, for example, chemical contamination was considered unimportant by most developing countries that had formulated these priorities in an explicit way (Johnson et al., 1977). In the same study, soil degradation and deforestation were identified as the two main environmental risks in a survey of 63 developing countries.

No doubt this will change now in view of the recent disasters in Mexico City and in Bhopal. Soil degradation, deforestation and drought continue to be top priority environmental problems; industrial and toxic pollution will be added to the perceived risk in many developing countries.

Third, an area that the conference may also want to examine is the path leading from research to development. It is assumed by many that research, like education, will lead more or less inevitably to socio-economic development. Experience in developed and developing countries, however, points out to significant exceptions to this equation. The contrasting situation in Japan and Britain in this respect is well known, the levels of research support being quite comparable in both countries, while the effects on economic development are very different. Ager (1985) has made the case for support of applied earth science research in developing countries. The important question here is: how well can one predict the translation of research results into socio-economic development? In Canada, some recent examples come to mind: mega projects - James Bay, Alberta tar sands, the northern pipeline; equivalent projects in the world are the large hydroelectric projects built in many countries in the last 25 years. Many of these have been severely criticised in a recent book by Adams and Solomon (1985).

In Ontario, there have been several attempts at targetting more specific areas of research: microelectronics and telecommunications and energy conservation, for example. Surprisingly, the emphasis on research in natural resource and environmental issues has been somewhat muted in recent years, in spite of the fact that geophysical companies, for example, fit very well in the pattern of the "threshold firms" identified in a Science Council of Canada study (Steed, 1982).

Good research facilities and experience in the natural resources field exist in Ontario universities, and at federal and provincial research organisations, as well as in many industrial laboratories in the province. Whether their experience is relevant to the needs of developing countries is something we continuously try to ascertain.

Fourth, the process of research cooperation is something that will affect the results of joint research projects. Although several Ontario universities have set up mechanisms to deal specifically with Third World development or development aid, carrying out a successful piece of research in the Third World depends ultimately on the same skills and knowledge that research everywhere is dependent upon. It is only that the issues are different, that the constraints act in different ways, and that the effects of one's actions may be quite more unpredictable than in a more structured society such as Ontario. We have enumerated some of these constraints as well as priorities for action in a separate brochure, and will welcome the opportunity to discuss them during the workshop.

LOCAL RESOURCES: POLICY CONSIDERATIONS

As understood here, local resources are those resources that are accessible to the local population with a relatively small technical and capital input, and for which there is an identified need or use in the immediate region concerned. These are, in one form or another, the traditional resources that poor rural populations have used for centuries, in some cases millenia: water, structural materials and most nonmetallic minerals. What is proposed here is to apply the arsenal of modern research tools to an understanding of these often neglected resources.

Among the advantages of this approach, we can list the following:

- Capital costs needed are usually smaller than for other types of resources (especially resources for export). This applies equally to exploration, exploitation, processing and transport.
- Advantages of scale are not too important; this means that exploitation and use can start at a small scale and proceed according to need.
- Generally labour intensive. Since the market is local, this means also that demand fluctuation can be anticipated more easily.
- Leading to development. Since these resources are put to use to build roads, houses, to provide irrigation, etc. they help to create a local infrastructure that improves the economy in a direct way; savings remain in the local community.
- Stepping stone to other technologies. Since most of the development of local resources is relatively simple, people can "graduate" to more sophisticated techniques after acquiring initial experience working in local resources.
- They respond to the main needs of the local population. Most of the local resources can be used to satisfy the primary needs of food, water and shelter. Their accessibility means also that people become more involved in their own process of development and in having more control over the local economy.
- Finally, these resources are generally safer to use. They are generally not very energy-intensive, their properties are well known to the users, most of them are stable materials with slow decomposition rates, and therefore pose relatively small environmental hazards.

REFERENCES

Adams, P. and Solomon, L. (1985) *In the Name of Progress*, Toronto: Energy Probe.

Ager, D.V. (1985) "Getting back to basics," *New Scientist*, February 21: 35.

Hart, D. (1980) *The Volta River Project: A Case Study in Politics and Technology*, Edinburgh: University Press.

Johnson, H., Johnson, J.M. and Gour-Tanguay, R. (1977) *Environmental Policies in Developing Countries*, Berlin: Erich Schmidt, Verlag.

Steed, G.P.F. (1982) *Threshold Firms*, Ottawa: Science Council of Canada Background Study 48.

PART II

BRIEF WRITTEN CONTRIBUTIONS

CHAPTER 5

EARTH SCIENCES AND ASSOCIATED PROCESSES AND
RESOURCES

THE GUELPH-MOROGORO AGROGEOLOGY PROJECT

Ward Chesworth
and
Peter van Straaten
Department of Land Resource Science
University of Guelph
Guelph, Ontario

Johnson M.R. Semoka
Department of Soil Science
Sokoine University of Agriculture
Morogoro, Tanzania

Jofephath Kamasho
Uyole, College of Agriculture
Mbeya, Tanzania

INTRODUCTION

Giving food aid to starving Africans means that the recipients can ⤳ eat for a while. But a long term solution requires an alternative to handouts. The ideal of course, is to help Africans to grow their own food. It is the ideal that fired the Green Revolution. Unfortunately, the high yield varieties of wheat and rice developed during the Green Revolution, require a western style infrastructure for their support and agrochemical inputs which particularly the poorest countries cannot afford. Introducing them to Third World countries demanded that local farmers give up traditional crops and techniques, no matter what the social cost, to become dangerously dependent on the alien husbandry of international agribusiness.

Parachuting a Saskatchewan farm on to an African landscape is not the answer. Africa can feed itself without such radical change. Arable soils exist and the best African farmers are at least as good as their North American counterparts at making the most of the soils that they have. African farmers have developed the requisite techniques to feed the continent on what has come to be called a minimum input basis.

Basically, minimum input agriculture requires soil, water, fertiliser, traditional crops and a relatively large labour force. Aid programs should focus on each of these resources and determine how best to optimise their use in a given farming community. The earth scientist has an important role to play in providing advice on the first three, and this paper focuses on fertiliser.

FERTILISER

Fertilisers are necessary, for when farmers remove a crop from the field they also remove nutrients stored within the plant material and ultimately obtained from the soil. This destroys any geochemical balance that may have existed in the landscape before farming began, and unless the nutrients are replaced, the soil will become less and less fertile with every succeeding crop. Plant and animal wastes in the form of compost and manure were widely used until the nineteenth century as soil additives to replace the deficient elements. The experiments of von Liebig ushered in the chemical fertilisers that have replaced these natural wastes in the agriculture of the developed world.

Commercial chemical fertilisers are formulations that contain one or more of the major plant nutrients N, P and K. N is obtained mostly from the atmosphere, though a small amount is geological in origin. P and K are derived almost exclusively from geological sources.

Clearly then, the geologist has an obvious part to play in locating deposits of P and K that can be converted into chemical fertiliser. Unfortunately, this would not greatly benefit subsistence farmers in Africa because the finished product is too expensive to buy.

For this reason, the University of Guelph and the Sokoine University of Morogoro in Tanzania have started a pilot project aimed at finding appropriate fertiliser raw materials for the farmers of the Mbeya district in southern Tanzania. The project is sponsored by IDRC, and will run for three years.

OUTLINE OF THE PROJECT

The project falls into three closely interrelated sections. First, we aim to locate geological resources available on a local scale, and useful as soil additives. Next, pot and field experiments will be performed to test their agricultural potential. Finally, an extension effort will be mounted to show local farmers the effects of each successful materials.

The materials we are concentrating on are liming materials, phosphatic rocks, volcanic scoria and zeolites.

Liming is necessary on many of the soils of the Mbeya region. Most are highly leached and are naturally acid. Some have become more acid by continuous application of ammonium sulphate fertilisers. A high acidity has the adverse effect of increasing the activity of Al and Fe in the soil so that these two elements fix phosphate ion and make it unavailable to an agricultural crop. Liming minimises this effect and both limestones and carbonates are available in the district to perform this function.

Phosphate rock is already being worked in northern Tanzania. In the Mbeya region, additional showings have been found in Songwe, Chamoto, Sengeri and Panda Hills. The Chamoto deposit is sedimentary in origin. The rest are apatite-bearing carbonatites. So far, our work - still in its early stages - has revealed new sedimentary deposits, northwest of Mbeya with greater than 12 per cent P_2O_5. One of our major difficulties has been to develop a geochemical technique useful in prospecting for these deposits. Our best results so far have been obtained by one of our co-workers, Peter Smith, who has modified the standard Shapiro technique by using sodium hydroxide solution to digest the sample. We will be testing this technique in Tanzania in the coming field season (Fall 1985).

Mbeya district contains a wide variety of volcanic rocks. We have collected scoriaceous types ranging from picritic basalts to phonolitic trachytes. Solution experiments now being performed at Guelph indicate that several of these have potential as a source of plant nutrients. And, unlike conventional fertilisers, they have the potential to supply a plant's minor element requirements as well as one or more of the major elements.

Zeolites are open structured framework silicates with large cation-exchange capacities. We have ion-exchanged a synthetic variety in the laboratory with 300 milliequivalents of NH_4+ ion per 100 grams. Natural, zeolite-bearing rocks collected in Tanzania gave values of about a third of this. We intend to use natural zeolites to fix ammonium in animal wastes and thereby provide a slow release nitrogen fertiliser. The ammonium-doped zeolite may also be useful in increasing the reactivity of rock phosphate when the two are mixed together.

THE FUTURE

The first agronomic experiments with the materials identified by us will begin this year in Morogoro under the direction of Dr. J.M.R. Semoka, the Head of Soil Science at Sokoine University. We are optimistic of the outcome for several reasons. First, the way the planet earth maintains soil fertility naturally is by adding fresh rock to the weathering system. Second, limestone, phosphatic rock and even volcanic scoria have been successfully used in direct application to agricultural soils in many parts of the world.

The potential is so great that during a meeting of the United Nations Economic Commission for Africa held in Lusaka, Zambia, from March 4 to 14, 1985, it was decided to set up an Agrogeology Network of which we will be an integral part. The main objective of this network will be to promote contacts between agriculturalists and geologists from participating countries, in order that the two groups can work together on farming problems for which geological expertise is required.

The network will include the following countries: Ethiopia, Uganda, Tanzania, Zambia, Angola and Mozambique, with Rwanda, Burundi and Malawi as additional possibilities. Workshops and seminars will be conducted in the various countries of East and Southern Africa in an attempt to propagate knowledge in this area and uncover new agricultural problems and areas where a geologist could help.

The ultimate objective is to encourage the search for agricultural raw materials in Africa, especially those of local significance, that can be used in the present framework of minimum input with the least possible disruption of the social fabric.

DEVELOPMENT, LANDSCAPE REDESIGN AND RESOURCE CONSERVATION

Using Earth Science Knowledge for Profit, Resource Conservation and Site Sensitive Planning Design

Alexander G. McLellan
Department of Geography
University of Waterloo
Waterloo, Ontario

In this brief article, an attempt is made to highlight various ways in which geomorphic knowledge can be used in a more ecological and integrative manner in development projects, especially in urban or near urban areas. Great opportunities exist for geomorphologists if they are prepared to become active in a wide-ranging series of issues relating to development and landscape change. Although most applications of geomorphic knowledge to such issues have been made in developed areas such as Canada and Western Europe, nowhere are such issues and needs more apparent than in the rapidly urbanising so-called Third World. Here there is frequently a lack of appropriate inventory mapping such as that possessed by the developed countries. Detailed soils, hydrologic, aggregate and other inventory maps and data are generally absent. Yet such data and the skills of the geomorphologist/planner are essential to the sound design, use and rehabilitation of surficial deposits in many different types of landscapes. These points will be illustrated briefly in the following paragraphs.

One of the most direct impacts of human activity is the creation of new landscapes through surface mining (Blunden, 1985). The widespread and large scale impact of this industry is very apparent in highly urbanised areas like southern Ontario. The aggregate industry is the largest user of land after agriculture and all combined urban uses. The search for aggregate deposits of suitable quality, quantity and location continues. In some areas with favourable near surface resource deposits, the use of aggregates has virtually overwhelmed all other considerations in the planning of landscapes. In such cases, geomorphologists cannot only provide accurate data on the quantity, quality and spatial distribution of deposits - including their location above and below the water table - but they can aid in planning and designing the reconstruction and use of mined areas (Yundt and Messerschmidt, 1979; McLellan et al., 1979; McLellan, 1981, 1985).

It has become apparent that rehabilitation should not be a post operative experience - an afterthought - in which one hopes to clean up the abuses of previous mining and related activities. Rather, rehabilitation should be planned, prior to the beginning of development activities, on the basis of knowledge of the character of the resources, the landscape in which they occur, surrounding landscapes and land uses, and future intentions of owners, users and government agencies in the region of concern. It is short-sighted to leave extensive derelict land around urban developments, airports, port installation, and other facilities located in highly visible situations. This is especially true for countries interested in foreign exchange earnings from tourism. A case in point is the huge government sponsored resort developed in the 1970s at Cancun in the Yukatan Peninsula, Mexico. Here the attractions of the new hotel strip and environs conflict with the dreary procession of highly visible non-rehabilitated quarries from which construction materials were derived - all located along main highway corridors.

Many landscapes are undergoing rapid change, or are planned to have dramatic change sometime in the future. Yet it has become quite clear that regardless of the success of new rehabilitation technologies and practices, the opening of new and somewhat incompatible land uses such as pits and quarries is not a pleasant prospect for many people. Despite the best attempts at innovative practice, the results often cause inconvenience for nearby residents. As a result, in the development of all new land in and around the urban periphery, we have developed what is called resource rescue. Thus, many of the landscapes in southern Ontario tend to be ones of fluvio-glacial deposition in which there exist quantities of sand and gravel that can be rescued during development. In one instance, an urban development site was lowered by approximately 20 feet and 2 1/2 million tons of sand and gravel were released for sale to a nearby aggregate producer. The removal of these aggregate materials was accomplished over less than five working seasons. An aggregate operation which was faltering because of resource exhaustion had its life extended several years. Indeed the operator is now using the same tactic on numerous other nearby resource-rescue development sites.

At another 20 ha site, an industrial subdivision was created above the regional flood plain after the removal of approximately 6 m of sand and gravel with a very high stone content (McLellan and Bryant, 1975). Below the regional flood plain line, the planned use after mining was to be scenic ponds and a picnic park beside a nearby river. Again, the overall plan was enhanced by a sensible use of geological/geomorphological information. As a result of such experiences, it is clear that geomorphologists can be effectively involved in many rapidly changing landscapes in certain areas. Developers, local governments, individual members of the public and society at large, can all be beneficiaries of wise use and rehabilitation of on-site and in-situ resources.

SUMMARY

The thesis of this article is that many landscape changes are taking place as a result of human activity. Some of these may be subtle, but many are not. It is suggested that geomorphologists have a major role in integrating their experience with those of other generalists and specialists who are guiding these changes. Indeed in many cases, the raw data which is fed into the decision making process is often derived directly from the field work and the field techniques of geomorphologists and those to which this information is most pertinent do not have the training to make the best use of it. Geomorphologists, therefore, have a responsibility to demonstrate their utility both here in Canada and in the Third World. Without this investment, mistakes will continue to be perpetrated and resource conservation opportunities lost. The geomorphologist acting in conjunction with a development team cannot only provide raw data, required for examination of a wider range of planning design decisions, but also can demonstrate and "flag" danger areas or profitable design alternatives. Development expertise learned through costly error and omission in Canada can help underwrite more efficient and less expensive development in the developing world.

REFERENCES

Blunden, J. (1985) *Mineral Resources and Their Management*, London: Longman.

McLellan, A.G. and Bryant, C.R. (1975) "The methodology of inventory - a practical technique for assessing provincial aggregate resources," *Bulletin of the Canadian Institute of Mining and Metallurgy*, 68(762): 102-8.

McLellan, A.G. Yundt, S.E. and Dorfman, M.L. (1979) *Abandoned Pits and Quarries in Ontario - A Program for Their Rehabilitation*, Toronto: Queen's Printer, Ontario Geological Survey, Miscellaneous Paper No. 79.

McLellan, A.G. (1981) "Rehabilitation - towards a wiser image of our land resources," in Mitchell, B. and Sewell, D. (eds.), *Canadian Resource Policies: Problems and Prospects*, Toronto: Methuen, pp. 180-208.

McLellan, A.G. (1985) "Government regulatory control of surface mining operation - new performance guideline models for progressive rehabilitation," *Landscape Planning*, 12: 15-28.

Yundt, S.E. and Messerschmidt, B.P. (1979) *Legislation and Policy, Minerals and the Environment Mineral Aggregate Resource Management in Ontario*, Vol. 1, Canada, pp. 101-116.

GORE-GAMBELLA GEOTRAVERSE PROGRESS REPORT

Calvin Pride
Ottawa-Carleton Centre for
Geoscience Studies
Ottawa, Ontario

INTRODUCTION

The Gore-Gambella Geotraverse project is a cooperative venture between the Ottawa-Carleton Centre (OCC) for Geoscience Studies and an Ethiopian group consisting of members from the Department of Geology at Addis Ababa University and the Ethiopian Institute of Geological Surveys (EIGS). It is funded mainly by IDRC with smaller contributions from UNESCO and CIDA. For several years, UNESCO has supported a program entitled "Geology for Development in Africa" to promote regional meetings of African geologists to establish a common understanding of regional research priorities and to finance related training courses. This particular project arose from an IDRC sponsored workshop held in Nairobi in May 1982.

The project was designed to study in detail, via 1:50,000 scale mapping, a representative cross-section of the Mozambique Belt, to:

1. understand better the geological evolution of the Belt including its potential for economic deposits;
2. strengthen the field and laboratory research capability of Ethiopian geological organisations, especially in highly deformed, metamorphic terrains;
3. create a favourable climate for scientific cooperation both between Canadian and Ethiopian partners and between geological groups in the different countries of the region where the geological environment is similar (e.g. Kenya).

To date, one field season has been completed and a second is in progress. Red tape and logistics have been the main problems. Preliminary results suggests little in the way of economic potential (geologically); but the training aspect of the project has been successful.

RATIONALE

The main features of the basement geology of eastern and northeastern Africa are two large scale structural elements of Precambrian age: the Nyanza Shield, composed of volcanic, sedimentary and granitic rocks of Archean age (2.5 - 2.8 x 10^9 years ago), and the Mozambique Belt, a complex, north-south trending metamorphic terrain to the east of the Nyanza Shield, formed by events of Proterozoic age (up to 0.5 x 10^9 years ago). The rocks of these ages that are exposed in western Ethiopia continue northward into Sudan and southward into Uganda, Kenya and beyond.

The genesis and emplacement of these rocks reflect major events in the history of the African continent. Their long evolution culminates at the end of the Precambrian time but their original composition and structure are hardly understood, as is the nature of the geological processes they record. As in other parts of the world where Shield rocks have been studied, a thorough understanding of these rocks depends not so much on characterisation of their composition as on the elucidation of their age and structural relationships.

Precambrian rocks everywhere are a major host of economic mineral resources. Important deposits of copper, iron, chrome, precious metals and stones are associated with Shield rocks in eastern and northeastern Africa, where these rocks are by far the main target for future mineral exploration. The discovery of future mineral deposits is crucially dependent on a good understanding of the geological evolution of the rocks that contain them. Geological mapping and interpretation, especially when they bring to bear on the problem the tools of modern geochemistry and structural analysis, are then an important prerequisite to sound geologic exploration.

The share of sub-Saharan developing nations in the word trade of mineral and ores has declined steadily since the 1950s. For Ethiopia in particular, mineral production has never been a substantial part of the economy. Geologically, however, the basement rocks which make up an important part of western Ethiopia are the very same rock types that account for most of the mineral production in some of the main mineral-producing countries of Africa and the world, and the expectation of this project is that ultimately, mineral production from Precambrian Shield rocks in Ethiopia will be made possible.

In some developing countries, serious economic imbalances are associated with heavy concentration on a small number of mineral commodities, or of oil. This danger is however, not an important one for Ethiopia, where the mineral sector of the economy plays a minor role. Although subject to the whims of world supply/demand patterns, minerals continue to be important in African economic and technological development. If maximum local benefit is to be derived from these resources, a country must develop the indigenous capacity to discover, evaluate and exploit mineral deposits. At the root of this process is the development of a group of competent earth scientists, in addition to sound university and geological survey infrastructures.

Before any plans can be made for the development of the mineral resources of the area, reliable information is needed on the distribution, size and value of these resources; this information is primarily derived from knowledge about the origin and evolution of the rocks where mineral deposits are emplaced. The Ethiopian government, through the EIGS, has set the detailed geological study of areas likely to be mineralised as a priority. However, due to lack of scientific staff with advanced training, this work cannot progress beyond the stage of generalised geological mapping, with a low interpretative content and a virtual absence of radiometric dates, petrologic studies and detailed structural analyses.

Two important requirements that need to be satisfied, therefore, are the development of a core of earth scientists competent to carry out the detailed studies mentioned above, and the strengthening of the appropriate geological survey and university infrastructures. The fulfillment of these two aims forms an integral part of this project.

GENERAL GEOLOGY

The area of the proposed geotraverse lies in Ilubabor Administrative Region of Western Ethiopia ($8^0 00'$ - $8^0 30'$ N: $34^0 30'$ - $35^0 45'$ E) it it comprises approximately 7,600 square kilometers covering 10 standard 1:50,000 map sheets (15' x 15'). The towns of Gore and Gambella are convenient reference points for the east and west ends of the geotraverse respectively. Over half of the project area is underlain by rocks of the Mozambique Belt, which are covered by volcanic rocks of Tertiary age in the east and by Quaternary alluvial deposits in the west. Geological reconnaissance mapping at 1:250,000 scale has been carried out in the area by EIGS;

immediately to the south, by a bilateral Ethiopia-Canada team (the Omo River Project) and to the north in Wollega Province by EIGS, United Nations and bilateral teams. Dr. John M. Moore, the leader of the OCC team, was senior participant in the Omo River Project.

Three Precambrian "domains" can be distinguished in the field area, based on variations in lithologic composition, structural style and degree of metamorphism. From west to east, these domains comprise:

1. migmatitic biotite gneisses and granitoid gneisses, with numerous pegmatite bodies; high grade metamorphic gneisses of sedimentary origin occur in the eastern part;
2. a low-grade metamorphic domain of volcanic and sedimentary origin, cut by granitic bodies; and
3. an eastern domain of high grade gneisses and migmatites.

These contrasting domains can be traced northward and southward, and constitute a major feature of the geology of western Ethiopia and adjacent parts of Sudan and probably Kenya and Uganda. Their relative ages and structural relationships, however, have yet to be determined. The gneisses and migmatites have been thought to be of Archean age, and the central·domain to be younger. However, rocks of the central domain bear a strong resemblance to some of the Archean rocks of the Nyanza Shield to the south and may therefore be actually the oldest. Solution of the problem of relative age of these domains would be a major contribution to the understanding of Precambrian geological evolution in all of northeastern Africa.

The area of the proposed geotraverse has been selected for the following reasons:

1. geological reconnaissance mapping has already been carried out in the area and in the adjacent terrain to both north and south. A variety of geological environments are represented, with a corresponding variety of mineral occurrences; base and precious metal deposits are known both in the study area and adjacent region;
2. geological features of the area extend into adjacent parts of neighbouring countries, and also have counterparts in other parts of Ethiopia. Data obtained during the project would therefore be applicable over a large region;
3. the area affords good accessibility without air support, by vehicle and foot traverses; rock exposures are adequate to

excellent. The area is secure, and numerous small settlements provide a measure of local assistance and supply.

TRAINING

Each field team consists of at least four members from OCC (faculty and research fellows) with at least an equivalent number of counterparts from Ethiopia. Assistance is provided where possible, by local students. Staff development is to be achieved by "in service" training during the cooperative mapping and follow up. In order to provide a measure of regional cooperation, provision is made for one graduate student and a faculty supervisor from Kenya to take part in the geotraverse (a reciprocal arrangement will be included in a planned proposal for a Kenya geotraverse). The two junior AAU faculty members who will come to OCC on postgraduate training will be supported by the fellowship program while in Canada. Their project-related travel will be funded by the project itself.

PROGRESS

The project is in its second of three years. One field season has been completed, and the second is in progress. The two Ethiopian graduate students have spent two terms in Ottawa. Laboratory work is underway, including dating of the rocks. Two map sheets and part of a third were completed in one year.

At this early stage, there is little in the way of progress regarding interpretation of the data at hand. Because of logistical, internal security and other problems, both field seasons took longer to get underway than anticipated and hence were shortened. From preliminary work, it appears that the rocks of this particular area have very little economic potential. This has been offset, at least partially, by the success of the training aspect of the project. It was discovered that the Ethiopian participants from the university had almost no field experience, particularly in deformed crystalline rocks, so that the field oriented project was of great benefit to them. The two Ethiopians working towards advanced degrees in Canada have outlined thesis projects and completed much of their course work.

Perhaps the main problem, and one found by relief organisations now active in Ethiopia, is logistical. Few roads and the nature of the terrain - a deeply dissected basalt plateau - make transport of camp and personnel very difficult and slow. The lack of water sources in the area further limit camp selection sites. Coping with these problems has been an educational and profitable experience for all project participants.

CHAPTER 6

WATER RESOURCES AND HYDROLOGICAL PROCESSES

RESEARCH ON EUTROPHICATION AND ITS APPLICABILITY TO FISH FARMING IN THIRD WORLD COUNTRIES

Jan Barica
National Water Research Institute
Canada Centre for Inland Waters
Burlington, Ontario

Eutrophication or enrichment of water bodies by plant nutrients, resulting in excessive growth of phytoplankton and macrophytes and impairing the use of water for recreation, water supply and fisheries, is a common problem in both developed and developing countries. While the solution to the problem is basically known (removal of excessive nutrients through advanced waste water treatment in municipal or industrial plants, changing agricultural practices to reduce basin runoff, etc.), its feasibility is questionable. The corrective measures are very expensive, require advanced technology and skilled manpower, and their success depends on the degree of dispersion of nutrient sources. The strategy to combat eutrophication in developed countries is to minimise nutrient input, and has proved highly successful in many countries, for example, the Laurentian Great Lakes, the Thames River, numerous European lakes and rivers.

In the Third World countries, however, where resources for this kind of capital-demanding expenditures are limited and overall priorities for their allocation are completely different, an approach to utilise the waste nutrients from population and agriculture to man's benefit should be applied. The two areas where this is feasible are irrigation and fish farming.

In this contribution, an example is presented of application of research results involving rainbow trout aquaculture from small prairie lakes in Canada to the fisheries of some countries in South-East Asia. The emphasis is on the prevention of massive fishkills which cause hardship to local fish farmers and may severely damage the whole industry.

RAINBOW TROUT AQUACULTURE IN CENTRAL CANADA

The research conducted by the Aquaculture Programme of the Freshwater Institute in Winnipeg during the 1970s developed a viable fish farming industry based on utilising the natural high productivity of small eutrophic lakes with abundance of benthic organisms to support growth of rainbow trout (Salmo gairdneri) from the fingerling size (3-4g) to about 300g within the ice-free season (April-October). As a rule, the survival rates have ranged from 0-85 per cent and the yields from 0-400kg/ha/season. Complete or partial summerkill or the mortality of trout following the collapse of an algal bloom (mainly *Aphanizomenon flos-aquae*) has been named as the major factor affecting survival. The mechanism of an algal bloom collapse in hypereutrophic lakes/ponds has been described in detail, and it has been concluded that the algae cause fish mortalities indirectly: it is their sudden death and subsequent bacterial decomposition which consumes all the oxygen in the water and this causes actual fishkills.

APPLICATION OF CANADIAN RESEARCH TO PREVENTION OF MASSIVE FISH MORTALITY IN SOME COUNTRIES OF SOUTH ASIA

The author had an opportunity to investigate and compare several incidents of massive fishkills outside Canada and found many similarities with the Canadian pattern. In South East Asia, these were:

1. Fish Mortalities in Laguna de Bay Fishpens (The Philippines)

Laguna de Bay is a major freshwater body located on Luzon Island. Aquaculture is practised here in fishpens, i.e. artificial enclosures constructed of bamboo stakes and fish netting, and represents about 40 per cent of the fish production through aquaculture. A major drawback of this convenient method for culturing milkfish (*Chanos chanos*, locally called *bangus*) are frequent fishkills, which vary considerably in severity from year to year. Frequently, about 700 ha of fishpens are affected and 5-6 million dead bangos reported. Value of fish lost is several million pesos. Unit rate of fish yield in lake is about 450 kg/ha and is sustained entirely by the natural biota of the Laguna de Bay which is similar to Canadian prairie lakes.

From the existing information and documentation of the 1975 fishkill as well as field observations by the author and application of his fishkill model from Canadian prairie lakes, it appeared to be primarily a collapse of a *Microcystis* bloom which causes milkfish mortalities in the Laguna de Bay fishpens. The collapse creates a nearly complete oxygen depletion in the water as a result of decomposition of dead algal cells on a massive scale. This process is further aggravated by high water temperatures resulting in low oxygen saturation levels. While the initial trigger of the algal collapse is not known, the author suspects sudden change in weather conditions, namely decrease in light intensity by heavy overcast. However, other causes such as salt water intrusion, stirring up the sediments by wind, clogging of fishpen netting and reducing water circulation, overstocking and overcrowding of fishpens, and pre-dawn oxygen depletion in certain areas, cannot be ruled out.

Despite striking similarities with summerkills in Canada and midwestern United States, no direct application of the results and conclusions on remedial activities under Philippine conditions could be made without studying the process on a scientific basis for a sufficient period of time. The critical limits for Laguna de Bay had to be established. Emphasis was laid on the possibility of signalling the approaching seasonal kill in the fishpens and saving the milkfish stock by harvesting it before the kill occurs, i.e. measuring biomass, dissolved oxygen and ammonia directly on site with basic field equipment.

2. Other Fishkill Mechanisms in the Region

Although the analogy between Canadian shallow pothole prairie lakes and Laguna de Bay fishpens was striking and the mechanisms of massive fishkills almost identical, other mechanisms are at work in polyculture farm ponds of the countries of the South China Sea Region.

For example, about 1,400 hectares of freshwater ponds in Hong Kong are producing a mixture of commercially important Chinese cyprinids and grey mullet. The culture system essentially conforms with traditional Chinese practices in small fertilised earthen ponds ranging from 0.3 to 1 ha each. The annual yields are high due to fertilisation and had a range from 2.5 to 5.5 tons/ha. The ponds are fertilised with rice bran, peanut cake, and manure from domestic animals.

About 30-40 per cent of the fish is believed to be lost through mortalities caused by oxygen deficiency during the months of July to

August. Fishkills are not total, however. The chlorophyll levels are in the range of 200-400ug/l, but occasionally rise to 700ug/l. *Scendesmus* and *Microcystis* are the predominant algal species. The lowest dissolved oxygen level recorded was 0.9mg/l.

It seems quite obvious that oxygen deficiency due to excessive growth of algae and their die-offs is responsible for fish mortalities again. The cause is similar to that in Canada and the Philippines, i.e. overproduction of algae and their adverse effect on water quality. Due to inadequate sampling frequency, it was not possible to establish whether the oxygen deficiency was total over a period of several days, or took place only for a short time in the early morning hours. The diurnal oxygen fluctuations in ponds at this latitude are known to be more significant than in Canada during summer months. This is a result of respiration by a heavy algal bloom during the night causing a temporary pre-dawn exhaustion of available oxygen, without an actual collapse of the algal bloom.

Similar description of partial fish die-offs have been reported throughout the Region (Thailand, Indonesia, Singapore). Since the ponds are artificially fertilised, increasing N/P rations in the fertiliser by either cutting down the P-rich components or adding more nitrogen-rich ones would likely improve the composition of the algal bloom, to favour more stable non-blue-green species.

THE RELATIONSHIP BETWEEN YIELDS AND WATER MANAGEMENT IN THE RICE INDUSTRY OF GUYANA

V. Chris Lakhan
and
Ihor Stebelsky
Department of Geography
University of Windsor
Windsor, Ontario

INTRODUCTION

In Guyana, water management, i.e. drainage, irrigation and flood control is a fundamental variable in the equation of efficient rice production. This paper examines the relationship between water management and yields in the rice industry in Guyana. Empirical investigations reveal that while yields may be influenced by several other parameters, for example, variety, husbandry practice and field sanitation, water management is the most critical variable.

RATIONALE FOR WATER MANAGEMENT

Rice production in Guyana is concentrated along the narrow 430 km coastal belt which is approximately 2.5 to 4 metres below high-tide level thus requiring an intricate network of sea defences, canals, sluices and other devices, to prevent salt water intrusion and to facilitate drainage, irrigation and flood control. In addition, land elevations delimit to a very significant extent supplies of water to rice cultivation other than that provided by gravity flow. Conversely, the coastal soils (comprising of 30-60 per cent clay, 30-60 per cent silt and less than 10 per cent sand) (Baskett, 1983) in the rice growing areas are characterised by low infiltration and permeability rates, necessitating drainage to prevent flooding in periods of heavy rainfall. Although rainfall can sometimes be excessive, rain-fed rice cultivation is not wholly feasible, given its precipitation patterns and intensity, water conservancy infrastructure, and rate of evapotranspiration.

THE RICE INDUSTRY

Rice is the largest privately cultivated crop in Guyana. It is the main source of food in the country and is the third largest earner of foreign exchange. Over the last 100 years, it has dominated all government land development schemes (Vining, 1975). Moreover, during the last three decades over 70 per cent.[1] of all government expenditures in agriculture has been devoted to water management beneficial to the rice industry. Figure 1 shows five of the seven major rice producing areas in Guyana. The other two areas, Leguan and Wakenaam, are islands in the Essequibo River. Each of the five demarcated areas benefits from a major water management project, each of which functions at varying degrees of efficiency depending on age of project, design, and maintenance of infrastructural works. The efficiency of the water management systems, in turn, determines rice yields.

RICE YIELD

Figure 2 shows that yields of paddy have fluctuated from almost 10 bags per acre to approximately 19 bags per acre during the period 1960-1981. Yields are based on production from harvested acreage. However, if yields were calculated from planted acreage they would be considerably less. For example, in 1961 and 1971 over 90 per cent of planted rice was harvested but in 1973 just over 60 per cent of planted rice was harvested. Empirical investigations [2] to ascertain the relationship between water management and yields revealed that farmers rightly calculated their yields based on planted acreage, since the necessary investment would have already been made. The results of the investigations further showed that over 95 per cent of the

----

[1] Government of Guyana, Annual Estimates of Expenditure, 1960-1981, and unpublished statistics, Planning Department, Ministry of Agriculture, Government of Guyana.
[2] Senior author conducted field surveys on the Essequibo Coast and Islands, East and West Demerara, and East Berbice and West Berbice.

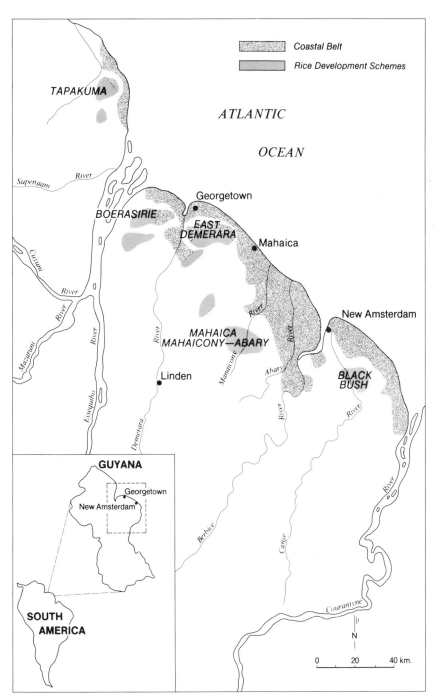

Figure 1: Main Rice Growing Areas in Guyana

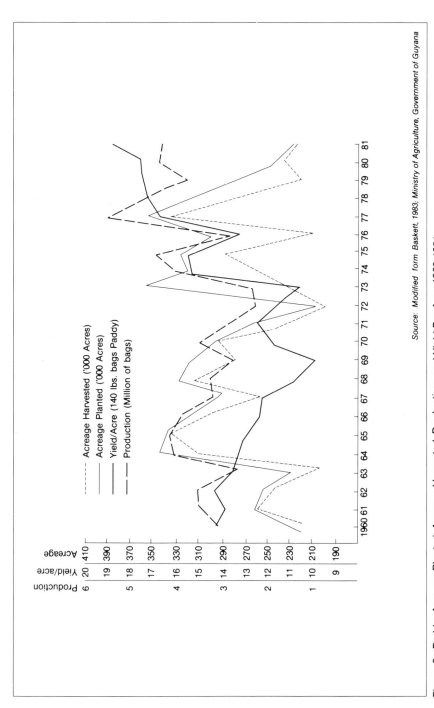

Figure 2: Paddy: Acreage Planted, Acreage Harvested, Production, and Yield Per Acre 1960-1981

Source: Modified form Baskett, 1983; Ministry of Agriculture, Government of Guyana

farmers did not harvest all or part of their unharvested cultivations as a result of insufficient or excessive water. This explains the difference between acreage planted and harvested in Figure 2. The results of the investigations attribute the difference to problems of irrigation (56 per cent) and drainage and flood control (39 per cent). These results are confirmed to a significant extent by an earlier study (Nathan, 1980) of the food crop sector which showed that over 50 per cent of all farm households in Guyana had a water management related problem. A later investigation (Hanrahan, 1982) revealed that 80 per cent of farmers encountered problems with drainage and flood control which significantly affected their yields.

Figure 2 also indicates that from 1961 to 1969 yields declined by almost 5 bags per acre. This period corresponds to decreased government expenditure in agriculture as a whole[3] and an accompanying deterioration of the water control infrastructure in the rice industry. Yields increased with government incentives during the country's 1972-1976 Plan period but fell significantly after planning expectations failed. However, with increased investment in water control (principally in the Tapakuma (TIP) and Mahaica-Mahaicony-Abary (MMA) areas), yields once again increased.

According to a Rural Farm Households Survey in Guyana (Nathan, 1980), farmers in the West Berbice area encountered the most significant water control problem while those in the West Demerara area had the least. An analysis of rice yields in those areas allude to the degree of efficiency of water management. This type of analysis can be applied to all the main rice growing areas but it should be noted that farmers in each of the areas cultivate many different varieties of rice (a subset of: BG79, D110, Rustic, Starbonnet, "N", IR22, Ledger), thus such an analysis is impractical. What is quite obvious from the survey results, however, is the fact that farmers in a particular area obtain different yields even though two farmers may be cultivating the same variety. The difference in yields can be attributed principally to the efficiency of water control whereby larger farmers purchase their own equipment to aid in water management. This is particularly evidenced in the Black Bush Polder area where yields using the same variety range from 12 to 23 bags per acre depending significantly on ownership or nonownership of water control equipment.

----

[3] Government of Guyana, Annual Estimates of Expenditure, 1960-1981, Georgetown, Guyana and Bank of Guyana Annual Reports, 1967-1971, Georgetown, Guyana.

The influence of water management on rice yields is further substantiated by the increases in yields after improving the water management infrastructure in the main rice growing areas. For example, in 1969, yield in both MMA and TIP areas was 8 bags (140 lb each) per acre (Vining, 1975). But improvements in water management in both areas, culminating in the completion of Phase 1 of both the MMA and TIP Water Management Projects, contributed significantly to yields increasing by 200 per cent and 300 per cent respectively, in the two areas by 1982.[4]

OTHER WATER RELATED PARAMETERS

The climate in Guyana is most suited for rice cultivation. Rainfall in the rice growing areas ranges from 80 inches in the Black Bush area to 100 inches in the Tapakuma area.[5] There are two rainy seasons, one of 120 days (mid-April to mid-August) and the other of 90 days (mid-November to mid-February), during which 50 per cent and 30 per cent annual rainfall occurs respectively. The remaining 20 per cent of annual rainfall is off-season. Given double cropping rice cultivation (spring and autumn), it could be concluded that more water would be required for the spring crop. While measurements of water requirements have not been made, it is evident from yield patterns in all the rice growing areas in Guyana that yields are higher in the autumn crop which is harvested after the longer of the two rainfall seasons.[6] This fact is more clearly brought out in comparing rice yields in the Wakenaam and Leguan areas which do not benefit from water management projects. For example, in 1982, spring crop yields in these two areas were 18.6 and 11.8 bags per acre respectively while autumn crop yields were 19.8 and 17.6 bags per acre.[7] Very significantly, during the spring months, farmers have to manage a greater volume of water, and in many cases, the water control facilities are inadequate. Hence, because of poor water management, yields in the Leguan area are generally lower during the spring crop

----

[4] Planning Department, Ministry of Agriculture, 1982, *Digest of Agricultural Statistics, 1975-1982, Annual Supplements*, Guyana.
[5] *Ibid.*
[6] Unpublished statistics on *Yield Trends in the Rice Industry, 1950-1980*, Planning Department, Ministry of Agriculture, Government of Guyana.
[7] Planning Department, Ministry of Agriculture, 1982, *op. cit.*

(Lakhan, 1972).

Another factor necessitating water management for rice cultivation in Guyana results from the high evapotranspiration loss which reaches 55 inches. Strachan (1980) claims that between 48-60 inches of irrigation water would be required to offset evapotranspiration loss and to meet additional water requirements, given the level of rainfall, if double cropping rice cultivation is practised. With a cropping intensity ranging from 1.4 to 1.7, this need may be less. However, other uses of water and wastage have to be considered in assessing water requirements of the rice industry in Guyana.

EVALUATION

The importance of water management to rice cultivation is established initially by the fact that over 70 per cent of all government expenditure in agriculture is allocated to water control beneficial to rice. Field investigations have confirmed that farmers see water management as the most important variable in determining yields in the rice industry. Cultivation and production trends indirectly point to the importance of water control, since increased cultivation is associated with increased government expenditure in water management. Increasing yields since 1976 have resulted from considerable improvement in the water management services in the rice industry. The fact that farmers who have water control equipment obtain higher yields, even though the same variety is being cultivated in the same area with similar soil, points to the crucial importance of water management in determining yields. The increases associated with adequately balanced rainfall confirm the need for increased water supplies to improve yields.

While this paper has sought to establish the relationship between water control and yields, it cannot be asserted to what degree water control influences yields. This becomes especially difficult since rice yields can be determined by several other variables including variety, fertiliser use, husbandry practice, field sanitation, soil condition, etc. The problem of estimating the individual contribution of any of the possible explanatory variables influencing yields was noted by Willardson (1974) who concluded that "increases that are uniquely due to drainage of agricultural lands are difficult to isolate because drainage is not the only factor in the production equation". Further, Behrman (1968), in examining the Thai rice industry, noted that although irrigation expansion may have been an important factor in the growth of Thai rice production, "data limitations direct statistical estimation of its significance". In comparison, the importance of water supply in Punjab to wheat yields was established by Gajri and Prihar (1983) and to yields of sugar beet in Italy by Barbieri (1982).

An important observation made in Guyana, however, which substantiates the importance of water control to yields is the fact that unharvested plantings have resulted from too little or too much water. While real yield may not rise if all the acreage cultivated were harvested, from a theoretical point of view, real yield would decrease if total production is calculated from total acreage cultivated, given the Guyanese situation. While this may be viewed as an indirect way of looking at the effect of water control on yields, it does demonstrate the fact that water management is important in increasing rice production in Guyana.

SUMMARY AND RECOMMENDATIONS

Field investigations revealed a direct relationship between water management and rice yields. This finding is supported by Baskett (1983), Strachan (1980), Vining (1975) and David (1969). However, smaller farmers (< 5 acres) who cultivate low-yielding traditional varieties which are more resistant to variations in climate conditions are not necessarily dependent on intricate water control systems. This can be partially explained by three factors:

1. maintenance of traditional cultures, using cultivation patterns (and varieties) proven successful in the past. Similar observations have been made in, for example, India (Lipton, 1982) and Thailand (Behrman, 1968);

2. the unreliability of the water control system and resulting losses to farmers have discouraged some farmers from cultivating hybrid (high yielding) varieties which require a controlled water supply for successful production;

3. the lack of acceptance of new varieties results from inadequate extension techniques to promote higher yielding varieties in several cases, thus negating the use of efficient water management.

An important derivative from this study is that farmers will select cropping patterns which suit their best interests, notwithstanding other parameters (in this case, efficient water control) which may increase their yields, and thus their incomes. This observation was made by agricultural planners in Guyana.[8] Moreover the investigations revealed that the effectiveness of the water control infrastructure is what determined productivity (synonymous with yields) in the rice industry and as such formed the basis of intensity of cultivation. In addition, the erasure of traditionality in rice cultivation can be facilitated by effective agricultural extension education and more significantly, by removal of the deficiencies in the water control system. It would be valuable to draw on the Chinese experience (Aziz, 1978) of traditionality versus modernisation and the resulting increases in yield, which was partially determined by improved water management.

The inefficiencies of the water control system in Guyana can be corrected by two mechanisms. Firstly, given the fact that the government does not efficiently maintain the water control infrastructure, a system of user-maintenance is recommended. This would service all farmers and would negate the inequalities resulting from the fact that all farmers in any specific area pay the same drainage and irrigation taxes. The revenues derived would be used to maintain efficiency in the system.

Secondly, for smaller farmers, and in areas where no major drainage and irrigation system exists, increases in yields can be effected by the provision of small scale irrigation equipment (for example, water pumps) to farmers. As recommended for India (Singh, 1984), research should also be conducted on land drainage systems which are suited to local conditions and needs. In addition, it will be worthwhile to practice irrigation farming, rather than wet farming, by transferring water from high volume reservoirs and basins to irrigate fields cultivated in the dry seasons.

REFERENCES

Aziz, S. (1978) *Rural Development: Learning from China*, New York: Holmes and Meier Publishers, Inc.

Barbieri, G. (1982) "Effect of irrigation and harvesting data on the yield of spring-sowa sugar beet," *Agricultural Water Management*, 5: 345-57.

----

[8] Ministry of Agriculture, 1983, *Directional Framework for Agricultural Development, 1983-1990*, Georgetown, Guyana.

Baskett, R.S. (1983) *Rice and Sugar in Guyana*, Washington, D.C.: Guyana Agricultural Sector Planning Project, Prepared under the Ministry of Agriculture/Checci and Company Contract, USAID Grant No. 504-0077.

Behrman, J.r. (1968) *Supply Response in Underdeveloped Agricultural: A Case Study of Four Major Annual Crops in Thailand, 1937-1963*, Holland: North-Holland Publishing Company.

David, W.L. (1969) *The Economic Development of Guyana, 1953-1964*, Oxford: Claredon Press.

Gajri, P.R. and Prihar, S.S. (1983) "Effect of small irrigation amounts on the yield of wheat," *Agricultural Water Management*, 6: 31-41.

Hanrahan, M.S. (1982) *Expanded Production of Foodcrops*, Washington, D.C.: Guyana Agricultural Sector Planning Project. Prepared under the Ministry of Agricultural/Checci and Company Contract, USAID Grant No. 504-0077, Washington, D.C.

Lakhan, V.C. (1972) "Transportation patterns in the Leguan rice milling industry," in *Occasional Paper No. 2*, University of Guyana, Department of Geography.

Lipton, M. (1982) "Game against nature: theories of peasant decision making," in Harris, I. (ed.), *Rural Development: Theories of Peasant Economy and Agrarian Change*, London: Hutchinsin University Library, pp. 258-68.

Nathan, R.R. Associates, Inc. (1980) *The Income and Production of Guyana Rural Farm Households: An Analysis Based on the 1979 Guyana Rural Farm Household Survey*, Washington, D.C.: Prepared for the Ministry of Agriculture, Government of Guyana and USAID under Contract No. AID-504-Inst.-781.

Singh, U.P. (1984) "Agricultural water resources management in India," *Journal of Water Resources Planning and Management*, 110(1): 30-8.

Strachan, A.J. (1980) "Water control in Guyana," *Geography*, No. 289, 65(4): 297-304.

Vining, J.W. (1975) "The rice economy of government settlement schemes in Guyana," *Inter American Economic Affairs*, 29 (Summer): 3-20.

Willardson, L.S. (1974) "Drainage for world crop production efficiency," in *Proceedings of the Contribution of Irrigation and Drainage to the World Food Supply*, New York: Specialty Conference American Society of Civil Engineers, pp. 9-19.

CHAPTER 7

FLOODING, TOXIC AND OTHER NATURAL AND ARTIFICIAL HAZARDS

HAZARDOUS WASTE (MIS)MANAGEMENT IN ONTARIO: SOME LESSONS FOR THIRD WORLD DEVELOPMENT

Murray Haight
School of Urban and Regional Planning
University of Waterloo
Waterloo, Ontario

In Canada and more specifically in Ontario, hazardous waste management issues are receiving considerable attention from the public, government, and industry. Generally speaking, these issues originate from two sources. In the first instance disposal practices of the past are creating problems today. Numerous (hundreds) of old landfill sites are now impacting surrounding environments and in some instances affecting human health. Leacheate plumes are migrating through underground aquifers - the same underground channels which serve as sources of water supply for nearby residents. The second source of the issues stem from problems being created as a consequence of activities underway today. Events arise because of accidents or upsets during the manufacturing process. Examples include the Junction-Triangle area in Toronto and Elmira, Ontario. Events also arise during the transportation of goods. Examples include the Mississauga train derailment and the spill of PCBs from a transformer being transported along the Trans Canada Highway in northern Ontario.

The issues are not unique to Ontario nor to Canada nor to North America but are increasingly being documented on a universal basis in both industrialised countries and in the less developed nations. In the latter instances "the situation is further compounded by what many in the Third World see as a double standards approach to the whole issue of chemical safety" (Mpinga, 1985). Chemicals which have been banned or restricted in Western Europe or North America are exported or manufactured and used in developing countries.

In the pursuit of hazardous waste management, numerous approaches, initiatives, and procedures are underway in Ontario. The efforts are about as diverse as the very nature of the issues themselves. In order to provide as meaningful a contribution as possible to those attending this conference, a case study has been selected and presented in terms of the problems, the concerns, the progress, and the lessons to be shared with others.

By way of further introduction it must be pointed out that the responses underway in most developed countries are by and large based upon public attitude. This began to shift essentially in the late 1960s and 1970s when environmental degradation as a result of man's activities came to the forefront of public attention. The realisation that man's unheeded "rape of the land" could lead to his ultimate destruction caused people to re-evaluate their perceptions and attitudes towards the environment. People realised that their environment was limited and vulnerable. The magnitude of environmental degradation caused by man's activities received mass media attention. The potential ill effects of chemical use on the environment and health, both over the short and long term, began to make headlines. In fact, the media were a prime force behind the upsurge in public interest in conservation and ecology.

Responses to the environmental crises of the 1960s and 1970s took the form of legislation and the creation of institutional arrangements designed to deal with environmental concerns. Environmental research became a governmental activity and an academic pursuit. A change in attitude occurred as land which had previously been viewed as a developable commodity came to be seen as a dynamic system. Environmental planning, based on this attitude change, began to evolve. The fundamental question which emerges for the Third World countries is whether or not the impetus for change will also originate because of public attention. If not, can the forces for change be expected to develop elsewhere?

CASE STUDY: PROPOSALS FOR THE REGULATION OF MOBILE PCB DESTRUCTION FACILITIES IN ONTARIO

Background

PCBs as a class of chlorinated aromatic hydrocarbons have been used extensively by industry and particularly by electrical equipment manufacturerers (Mpinga, 1985). During the late 1960s concerns were raised about environmental and health impacts. Eventually production was halted and regulations were developed on their use and disposal. In addition to the toxic effects of PCBs themselves, sensitivity towards their storage and destruction has increased and is partially based on the evidence that in some instances dioxins and furans may be present.

Associated with the ban on the use of PCBs and because of the impossibility at present to destroy the wastes, the need developed in Ontario to locate and design safe and secure storage facilities. In 1979 the Ontario government instructed a consulting firm to select appropriate site(s). The Ontario Ministry of the Environment (MOE) selected one but it was largely because of opposition raised by the local community that the proposal was eventually withdrawn. One of the major issues the community group argued was that as an alternative to trucking waste materials to a central storage facility, the Ministry should assess the feasibility of using mobile destruction facilities. In that way the PCB waste would be destroyed at sites where the materials were already deposited. Attempts to establish permanent destruction facilities were also unsuccessful - again largely due to local public opposition and again the issues surrounded centralised versus decentralised approaches.

Current Activities

At present interim storage of PCB wastes is permitted and regulated under the Environmental Protection Act. What is being established is temporary on-site storage and the intent is to store all wastes at points of generation. The regulations also provide for some movement of PCB waste to and from the sites.

In the meantime the MOE is supporting the option to establish mobile PCB destruction facilities as a method of addressing the disposal problem in Ontario. The process to secure the necessary approvals is elaborate and extensive. This is because if the current approval processes as applied for the operation and siting of fixed facilities were applied to the mobile concept, a public hearing and possibly an environmental assessment would be required for each new siting. The MOE has undertaken to submit to public hearings held by a commission constituted under the Public Inquiries Act. To complete its task the MOE has assumed the role of a proponent and submitted a proposal outlining a regulatory and administrative framework. An extensive public consultation program has allowed input into the development of the approvals process as well as for the concept of using mobile facilities. The hearings are just over and the commission is currently preparing its recommendations.

Lessons for Others

Since the initial ban on the use of PCBs over a decade ago very little progress seems to have evolved to address the issue of safe destruction; that is until very recently when the latest efforts have been initiated by the Ontario government. The desire to proceed is shared by everyone as they face the increasing risks of contamination. The effort seems to reflect a unique approach in at least two regards; the concept of mobile destruction facilities travelling to various communities will be in lieu of the alternative which is traditionally to truck the wastes to a central facility. Also the government is acting both as the proponent during the public hearing process as well as the regulatory agency in supplying the criteria, standards, and guidelines for emissions, handling, and safety procedures. These latter functions will extend when the MOE grants approval to various operations and then subsequently routinely monitors their operations.

The processes to gain final approval and to administer, once approval has been achieved, are complex. All levels of government are involved. The pieces of legislation extend from the Environmental Contaminants Act, Transportation of Dangerous Goods Act of the federal government to the Environmental Assessment Act, Environmental Protection Act, Dangerous Goods Transportation Act, Occupational Health and Safety Act, Ontario Water Resources Act of the provincial government, to various by-laws and other legislations under the Planning Act and Public Health Act at the level of the regional or municipal governments. The possibility cannot be ignored that jurisdictional difficulties such as duplication, overlap, or gaps will likely exist. Applying the management assessment framework presented in the overview paper by Nelson and Knight (1985) (see

Chapter 1) should assist in evaluating this and other aspects related to the planning implementation and monitoring of facilities.

One of the advantages of attempting to develop regulations for mobile destruction facilities in Ontario is the basic fact that provincial standards or guidelines currently exist for many of the emissions into the environment. In other jurisdictions, including many other parts of Canada, such benchmarks do not always exist. Michaels *et al.* (1985) have suggested that "in the area of standard setting, the development of a uniform, international set of permissible exposure levels would be extremely helpful . . . Internationally accepted standards are less likely to be compromised by local economic interests and more likely to be based on solid scientific data". Recent efforts by the InterAmerican Center for the Study of Social Security, and the United Nations' initiated International Programme on Chemical Safety are attempting to address some of these issues.

Whatever specific mobile facilities are approved, they will employ sophisticated technology not only in terms of the process equipment itself but also to monitor various emissions and other by-products. Few proponents and few others have the expertise, the equipment, or the capital to be able to meet the stringent criteria being proposed. The role of experts to assist in various facets of the development and application becomes a critical aspect.

The emphasis developed for the hearings has been to propose that a facility be allowed to operate at any approved site. This would occur after careful evaluation had been completed on the performance of a facility. The hearing process has, by its very nature, attempted to secure the opinions from all sides, including the public. When all is said and done and approval is eventually granted, public acceptance of a facility in a specific community will still possibly remain a contentious issue. It is the one key aspect which will require close attention if the concept is to move towards reality. If everything is eventually accepted and the processes prove successful in safely destroying PCB materials, then one cannot overlook the eventuality that other types of hazardous materials could be managed in a similar fashion.

CONCLUDING SUGGESTIONS

In Ontario hazardous waste management is currently a high priority. What is underway represents the culmination of a number of features pertaining to Ontario. The attitudes and perceptions of the public, government, and industry are generally supportive that something must be done. The state of the environment including the social, economic, political, and physical dimensions are also appropriate for efforts to be undertaken. But what about the cultures, the idiosyncracies, and levels of development in other countries - are they all combined in such a fashion that efforts similar to what is occurring in Ontario would be likely to be implemented? In many developing nations, however, the major health concerns are the by-products of underdevelopment to which have been added the results associated with industrialisation.

Perhaps now is the time to begin to focus on efforts that are truly reflective of the situations existing in specific Third World countries. A practical suggestion would be to begin to look at each situation in much the same fashion as ecologists examine the elements and processes at work within an ecosystem. In the ecosystem concept, for example (see the work by Odum and others reviewed by Nelson and Knight) in their overview paper (Chapter 1) the emphasis is upon the system as a whole at work and where alterations or impacts in one part are likely to affect all other parts as well. As a first step it would be necessary to identify the elements and processes. Mendes (1985) has provided a partial list of a number of "determinants" which fall into three categories. The first group comprises a number of general determinants including the economic organisation, living conditions, social security schemes, educational and training opportunities. The second category termed the labour structure includes the work organisation and opportunities, union labour organisation, legislation and enforcement, and the science and technology available. The final category is the health sector and takes into account the "normal" distribution of health and disease, the health care system, the influence of biological and social characteristics, and the risks associated with different lifestyles. Once such a system is defined it would be possible to evaluate the potential costs and benefits likely to occur with the allocation of limited resources. Perhaps some of these suggestions will be addressed in the workshops which are to follow in this conference on "Research for Third World Development".

REFERENCES

Mendes, R. (1985) "The scope of occupational health in developing countries," *American Journal of Public Health*, 75(5): 467-68.

Michaels, D., Barrera, C. and Gacharna, M. (1985) "Economic development and occupational health in Latin America: new directions for public health in less developed countries," *American Journal of Public Health* 75(5): 536-42.

Nelson, J.G. and Knight, K.D. (1985) "Ontario research, resources and environment in the Third World - a workshop introduction and overview," prepared for the Conference on Research for Third World Development: Ontario Perspectives, Waterloo: University of Waterloo.

Mpinga, J. (1985) "Controlling the chemical threat," *The IDRC Reports*, 14(1): 21-2.

Mpinga, J. (1984) *Preliminary Hearing Document on Proposals for the Regulation of Mobile PCB Destruction Facilities in Ontario*, Toronto: Ontario Ministry of the Environment.

PROBABILITY STUDIES OF FLOODS [1]

Ming-ko Woo
Department of Geography
McMaster University
Hamilton, Ontario

Peter R. Waylen
Department of Geography
University of Saskatchewan
Saskatoon, Saskatchewan

INTRODUCTION

Floods and droughts are hazards which recur at various magnitudes and intervals. On a short term basis, they are related to the meteorological elements and the soil and groundwater storage conditions that prevail at a particular time and at a certain locale. Day to day hydrological forecasting techniques are well developed to reduce the economic and human impacts of these hazards. Economic and land use planning on a regional scale, however, requires a prediction of the long term pattern of the hydrological regime. Statements pertaining to the probability of occurrence of floods and droughts are the requisite information.

----

[1] Financial support is provided by research grants from the Natural Science and Engineering Research Council of Canada. This work is part of the McMaster University Research Program for Technological Assessment of Subarctic Ontario.

Where there are long records available, it is straightforward to abstract from the data the probabilities of various flood and drought characteristics. In many parts of the world, data are sparse. Either many stations have been in existence for only a short time, or many areas are not covered. Northern Ontario is one such region which has few hydrometric and climatic stations, many of which have no more than 20 years of record. The experience gained in analysis of the floods and droughts of this region can therefore be applied profitably to other parts of the world confronted with similar data limitations. This paper outlines two approaches that extract flood information from the short records so that the long term probability structure can be determined; the paper also describes a well known geographical technique with which such probability estimates can be extended to the ungauged areas in the region. Treatment of droughts will not be included because of the shortage of space.

NORTHERN ONTARIO BASINS

Rivers in northern Ontario drain into Hudson Bay and James Bay. Total drainage area exceeds 400,000 (km² and is equivalent to the combined area of the United Kingdom, Ireland, Denmark, Belgium and Holland. Yet, this vast region is served by only 46 stream gauging stations, a density equivalent to having 28 gauges to cover the entire United Kingdom. Such a low network density is quite similar to those found in parts of the developing world.

Topographically, the lower basins occupy lowlands which are underlain by Palaeozoic sedimentary and volcanic beds (Figure 1). Poor drainage produces extensive wetlands. The upper basins rise to 500 m and they occupy the Canadian Shield, with temperate forests covering extensive areas. The western sector is dotted with lakes in a rolling landscape, while the southern fringe is a plateau with pockets of farmland. The region is largely underdeveloped, with trapping and fishing being the primary human activities in the north, and mining, logging and farming being important in the south (Hutton and Black, 1975).

Other than a narrow strip fringing the Hudson Bay which has an arctic climate, the region lies in the boreal climatic zone (Hare and Thomas, 1974). It is characterised by harsh winters with a mean January temperature of -25°C at the coast, increasing to -17°C in the south. Summer temperatures are spatially more uniform. Annual precipitation increases southeastward, from 500 mm at the Manitoba border to 800 mm at the Quebec border. Snowfall is important

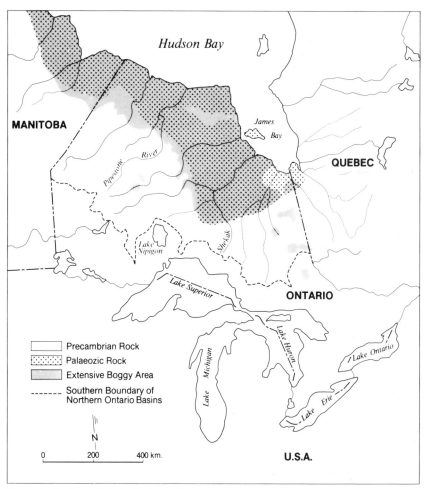

Figure 1: Northern Ontario Drainage Basins

between November and March, and snowmelt often begins in April. Many areas experience snowmelt flood and winter low flow when freezing conditions prevail. In other parts of northern Ontario, multiple floods occur due to spring melt and summer or autumn rainfall. Multiple low flows can also occur because of winter cold and summer water loss due to more intense evaporation. The presence of multiple peaks and multiple low flow events are analogous to those of the monsoonal and some tropical areas where the inter-tropical convergence zone sweeps frequently across the land.

ESTIMATING HIGH FLOW PROBABILITIES

Floods and droughts imply human suffering, environmental damages and economic losses not readily apparent in the hydrological data. Yet, the dimension of these hazards must be quantified to permit statistical predicting which in turn allow preventive or protective measures to be adopted. For this purpose, specific levels of streamflow are taken as surrogates for stages above which damaging floods occur; or below which the impacts of drought, are felt. Thus, in the following analysis, high and low flows are considered to be indicators of floods and droughts.

Traditionally, the largest daily discharge in a year (annual flood) has been selected for study (Darlymple, 1960). A certain probability distribution is chosen to model the magnitude of flow. Examples include the gamma, Pearson Type 3, extreme value and log distributions (National Environment Research Council, 1975). Generally, the criterion for adopting a particular distribution is that of best of fit. When a distribution has been identified as appropriate, the parameters are estimated from the available data which represent a limited sample. Using these parameters, the entire distribution is generated. In many instances, the annual floods are caused by one single hydrological process such as snowmelt. If the floods are due to a mixture of processes (e.g. floods in some years are produced by snowmelt, and in other years by rainfall) a compounded probability distribution is required to describe the flood events drawn from distinctly different populations.

As examples, the probability distributions of Shekak and Pipestone rivers in northern Ontario are presented. The basin areas are 3,290 and 5,960 km^2 respectively. In the former case, all annual floods are due to snowmelt alone, and the Gumbel distribution can satisfactorily represent the probability distribution:

$Prob\ (Annual\ flood \leq given\ value\ of\ z\ m^3/s) = \exp\{-\exp[-\alpha(z-\beta)]\}$

where the two parameters α and β are estimated from the sample mean ($\bar{z}$) and sample standard deviation (s) of annual floods:

$\alpha = 1.281/s$ and $\beta = \bar{z} - 0.45s$

The continuous line in Figure 2 shows the resultant Gumbel distribution. For Pipestone River, annual floods are generated by two processes (rain and snowmelt) and a compounded Gumbel with four parameters is required. The method is described in Waylen and Woo (1982) and the results are shown as the dashed line in Figure 2. When the probability distribution is determined, the probability of annual floods exceeding any magnitude can be predicted. For instance, the probability of annual floods exceeding 300 m³/s is 0.3 for Pipestone River and it is 0.1 for Shekak River.

The above analysis has practical limitations when more than one damaging flood occurs each year. For planning purposes, it may be desirable to know the frequency, magnitude, duration and the timing of different flood events. In this case, the analysis of the partial duration series is appropriate (Todorovic, 1978). The definition of floods will include all daily discharges exceeding some level of concern (Figure 3). The relevant variables include the number of such floods per year, the time and duration of their occurrence and the maximum flow the river attains during any such period. The probability distributions used to describe these variables have a theoretical foundation and the parameters can be estimated from a limited number of years of flow record.

As an example, the partial duration series of Shekak River (19 years of data available) is given below. The number of floods per year follows a Poisson distribution and their magnitude and durations are exponentially distributed. The dates when each flood begins are normally distributed, with a mean data and a fixed variance that describes the year to year variability in the timing of flood events. The statistical techniques employed are given in Waylen and Woo (1983) and only the results will be discussed to show the information obtainable from the analysis. In the example, all of the high flows exceeding 200 m³/s are considered to be hazardous. The occurrence of such floods averages 0.63 per year and the probability of having 0, 1, 2, . . . number of such floods per year is shown in Figure 3b. Each of these floods last 10.7 days on the average, and the probability of various durations is presented in Figure 3c. The magnitude of

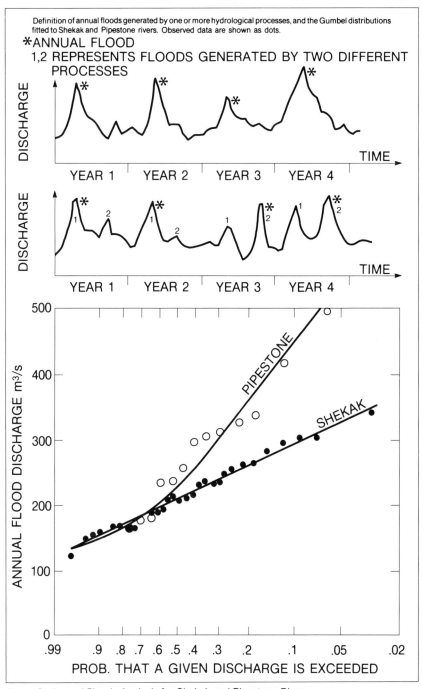

Definition of annual floods generated by one or more hydrological processes, and the Gumbel distributions fitted to Shekak and Pipestone rivers. Observed data are shown as dots.

Figure 2: Annual Floods Analysis for Shekak and Pipestone Rivers

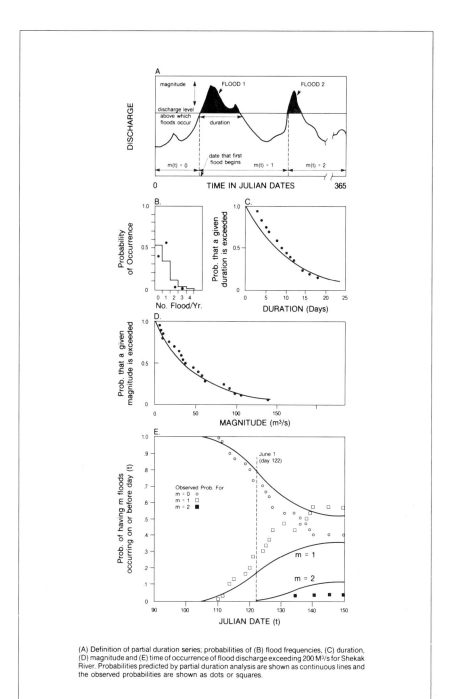

(A) Definition of partial duration series; probabilities of (B) flood frequencies, (C) duration, (D) magnitude and (E) time of occurrence of flood discharge exceeding 200 M³/s for Shekak River. Probabilities predicted by partial duration analysis are shown as continuous lines and the observed probabilities are shown as dots or squares.

Figure 3: Partial Duration Analysis for Shekak River

floods averages 49.4 m³/s above the critical high flow level and the accompanying distribution is given in Figure 3d. Figure 3e shows the probabilities of having no flood, or m(t) = 0; one flood, or m(t) =1, two floods and etc. on or before day t. For instance, by Julian day 122 (June 1), the probability of not having any flood at all is 0.78, the probability of having one flood is 0.16, and having two floods is 0.03.

Partial duration series analysis can be extended to include high flows generated by more than one hydrological process. The Pipestone River can be taken as an example because its high flows are caused by snowmelt and rainfall. Regardless of whether the floods are due to a single or a mixed generating processes, once the suitable probability distributions are identified and the pertinent parameters estimated from the relatively short streamflow record, the probability of occurrence of various attributes of flood events can be obtained.

SPATIAL INTERPOLATION OF FLOOD PROBABILITIES

For many basins without streamflow records, it is possible to make use of the parameters derived from the entire region to estimate parameter values for the ungauged basins. One way to represent the spatial variation of the parameters is by trend surface fitting, a method well tested in geographical and geological research (Krumbein and Graybill, 1965). This method uses the spatial coordinates (such as longitude and latitude) of the basin centroid as independent variables with which to estimate the parameters. The assumptions are that the spatial variation of the parameter values can be described by the trend surface; and that the basins are not so large that the parameters estimated for the centroid are representative of the entire basin.

As an example, the surfaces representing the mean annual floods due to snowmelt and rainfall are shown as three-dimensional plots in Figure 4 (Woo and Waylen, 1984). These surfaces were obtained by first estimating the parameters for individual stations scattered in northern Ontario where streamflow data are available. Then, the parameter values were used to derive third-order trend surface equations using least-square fitting. The trend surface equations are expanded to solve for the whole of northern Ontario so that parameter values can be interpolated for any point in the region where streamflow data are not available. Once the parameters are calculated, it will be possible to predict the probability of occurrence of various flood characteristics.

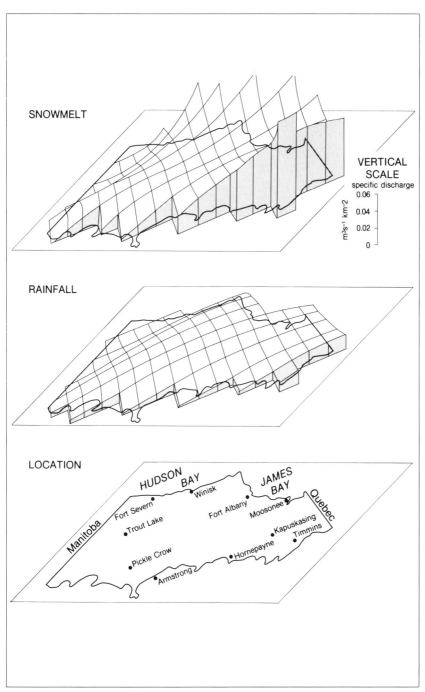

Figure 4: Areal Variation of Mean, Annual Maximum Flows Due to Snowmelt and
          Rainfall in Northern Ontario

DISCUSSION

Although limited space precludes discussions on droughts, both floods and droughts are extreme events which exhibit similar statistical properties. Some methods suitable for flood analysis may be applied to droughts when appropriate modifications are made. Similarly, heavy rainstorms and climatic droughts - as distinct from low flows - can be treated by the techniques described.

The results presented in this paper pertain to natural streamflow regimes. The probability distributions will inevitably be altered when the basins or their rivers undergo substantial man-made changes. These hydrological impacts should also be studied probabalistically to assess the effectiveness of the projects or to determine the long term effects on the environment.

The methods outlined in this paper are well suited to regions where data are sparse. The usefulness of these methods have been demonstrated for northern Ontario. The same approaches can be applied to analyse the hazards of floods and droughts in the developing countries. The information thus obtained will facilitate the rational planning and proper utilisation of the water resources in these parts of the world.

REFERENCES

Darlymple, T. (1960) *Flood Frequency Analysis*, Washington, D.C.: U.S. Geological Survey Water Supply Paper, 1543-A.

Hare, F.K. and Thomas, M.K. (1974) *Climate Canada*, Toronto: John Wiley and Sons.

Hutton, C.L.A. and Black, W.A. (1975) *Ontario Arctic Watershed*, Ottawa: Lands Directorate, Environment Canada, Map Folio No. 2.

Krumbein, W.C. and Graybill, F.A. (1965) *An Introduction to Statistical Models in Geology*, New York: McGraw Hill.

Natural Environment Research Council (1975) *Field Studies Report*, Vol. 1, Hydrological Studies, Wallingford, United Kingdom: Institute of Hydrology.

Todorovic, P. (1978) "Stochastic models of floods," *Water Resources Research*, 14: 345-56.

Waylen, P.R. and Woo, M.K. (1982) "Prediction of annual floods generated by mixed processes," *Water Resources Research*, 18: 1283-86.

Waylen, P.R. and Woo, M.K. (1983) "Stochastic analysis of high flows in some central British Columbia rivers," *Canadian Journal of Civil Engineering*, 10: 205-13.

Woo, M.K. and Waylen, P.R. (1984) "Areal prediction of annual floods generated by two distinct processes," *Hydrological Sciences Journal*, 29: 75-88.

CHAPTER 8

COASTAL AND FRESH WATER LAKE DEVELOPMENT AND CONSERVATION

REFORM SUSTAINABLE REDEVELOPMENT OF THE NORTH AMERICAN GREAT LAKES

Henry A. Regier
Institute for Environmental Studies
University of Toronto
Toronto, Ontario

George R. Francis
Department of Environment and Resource Studies
University of Waterloo
Waterloo, Ontario

INTRODUCTION

This paper is based on reflections from our collaborative work with a number of people in Canada and in the United States on issues of Great Lakes redevelopment. By "redevelopment" we mean the investment of substantial sums of money for the rehabilitation of badly degraded ecosystems so that they may once again provide for the sensitive beneficial uses consistent with a healthy developed society.

It may be a theme of increasing interest to colleagues in the Third World whose responsibilities for resource and environmental management are essential components of natural or subnational regional development. With hindsight examination of the situation in the Great Lakes, we would strongly emphasise the importance of taking preventive measures against degradative exploitation of environmental resources wherever there is still an opportunity to do so. Fortunately, this realisation is being acknowledged globally, as evidenced by the IUCN's World Conservation Strategy document and other advocates of ecologically sustainable development practices.

While the Great Lakes may be unique as the world's largest set of freshwater resources, their history of abuse and degradation is not unique. Recent exchanges of information with European colleagues revealed comparable experiences and conditions in the Baltic Sea. We have been made increasingly aware that the Great Lakes situation is only one among many examples of the increasing scale and complexity of human impacts on environmental resources over whole regimes. This phenomenon testifies to the urgent need to rethink what is to be done in the name of "development", and to the urgent need to devote much more research effort on questions of ecologically sustainable development practices.

CONVENTIONAL ECONOMIC DEVELOPMENT

The North American Basin of the Laurentian Great Lakes may usefully be compared with the European Basin of the Baltic Sea. The Baltic Sea is somewhat larger but this difference does not invalidate some comparisons.

Both regions are bordered in the north by the eroded granitic base of an ancient mountainous region which was continuous before the continents migrated apart. The most southerly parts of the basins have areas of fertile, deep, well watered soils due in part to depositions by repeated glaciation in recent geological history. The climate is temperate. The large water bodies central to the basins have been important in the industrialisation of the past two centuries, and have responded to its abuses.

Since about 1860, the histories of development in the two Basins have similarities. The natural endowment of the two Basins was quite similar both with respect to renewable and nonrenewable resources. The human culture that dominated both Basins during this period was very similar, in part because the Great Lakes Basin was conquered and settled by people of Northwest Europe, i.e. from the Baltic Basin and adjacent regions. The parallels in commercialisation, industrialisation and urbanisation were quite similar. Overall, the culture of the Baltic was less destructive of the natural parts of the ecosystem during peace times, but more destructive during war times - so, on balance, the level of destructiveness of the people of the two Basins has not differed greatly.

By 1960, the legacy of all the "modernisation" of the preceding ten decades was comparable in the two Basins. Water bodies - from small streams to rivers to estuaries to some nearshore waters of the brackish Baltic and of the freshwater Great Lakes - were strongly modified and often severely polluted. Cities were dirty and their industries polluted the air which was transported long distances to cause acid rain and toxic fallout which degraded the sensitive lakes and forests. Some fertile lands were eroded away, others were coverted to urban settlements and transportation corridors. And so on.

By the late 1960s it was difficult for informed people to evade the realisation that the cultures of the general regions of the Great Lakes and the Baltic were highly destructive of the natural resources, and of the more desirable attributes of the human culture. This led to the reconsideration of conventional economic development as in FAO's Second World Food Congress at The Hague in 1970, the attempt to develop international consensus on remediation of environmental abuse as at the 1972 Stockholm Conference on the Human Environment, and the initiative of UNESCO's Man and the Biosphere Program to develop understanding appropriate to ecosystem husbandry. These and related initiatives implied that the conventional exploitive development, CED, that emerged in western culture needed to be reformed drastically, say in the direction of sustainable redevelopment.

The regions of western Europe and northeastern North America where CED flourished - apparently successfully for some ten decades - was comparatively resilient to the destructiveness of CED. If CED could not succeed here, there was little prospect that it could succeed in regions that were naturally and culturally less rich and resilient with respect to ecosystem features. Most of the rest of the world falls in a category of being less resilient. Thus it was widely recognised by the late 1960s that CED could not succeed to improve the lot of the world's people, in the long run. That CED could not even be relied on to improve the well being of the people of the Great Lakes was also recognised at the time. Since then we have tried to reform our ways, as sketched below.

We focus here on the Great Lakes themselves as integrators of the abuses of our culture. In recent decades, the Great Lakes have been affected by the abuses that originate not only in the Basin itself, but from far beyond it, as with pollutants transported atmospherically.

CULTURAL ABUSES OF GREAT LAKES ECOSYSTEMS

Within CED, many initiatives that were taken to improve the lot of some groups of humans had serious adverse consequences to the more desirable features of the natural part of the ecosystem, and to the direct users of those more desirable features. Table 1 shows a listing of those with serious effects on the Great Lakes, and especially on their fisheries.

When these abuses became intense and/or when more than one kind was applied to the same part of the Great Lakes, then a kind of ecological slum resulted. The "ecosystem degradation syndrome", EDS, that ensued with respect to the aquatic part of the Great Lakes Basin usually had the following characteristics:

The major ecological stresses associated with human uses as conventionally practiced at levels of some intensity often act synergistically so as to exacerbate each other's adverse effects and seldom act antagonistically so as to cancel out adverse effects.

The stresses separately and jointly act to alter the fish association from one that is dominated by large fish usually associated with the lake bottom and lake edge to one characterised by small short-lived mid-water species. A similar change happens with respect to vegetation, from firm rooted aquatic plants originally in the near shore to dense suspensions of open-water plankton algae. Further, the association of relatively large benthic invertebrates directly on bottom, such as mussels and crayfish, is supplanted by small burrowing insects and worms such as midge larvae and sludge worms. Broadly similar changes occur in the flora and fauna of the wetlands and nearshore areas bordering these waters.

With the above changes comes an increased variability from year to year in abundance of particular species, especially of landings of different fish species by anglers and commercial fishermen. Fluctuations are also more pronounced in the species associations of wetland, benthic and pelagic areas.

The shift from large organisms associated with the edges and the bottom of the waterbody to small organisms in the bottom mud and mid-water is not accompanied by a great

Table 1

A Taxonomy of Stresses that Affect Aquatic Ecosystems of the Great Lakes

Natural background processes	Battering storms; rains and floods; water level cycles; spells of hot or cold weather; forest and marsh fires; disease outbreaks.
Harvesting of renewable resources	Fishing whether commercial, angler or by party boat, hunting for ungulates, upland birds or waterfowl; trapping for muskrat or fox; withdrawal of water for consumption.
Loading by substances and heat energy	Inert solids and suspensions of sand and clay; nutrient materials that fertilize plants and plankton; poisons that kill organisms; contaminants that affect health of organisms; heat that raises the temperature of the water.
Restructuring the morpho-metric form of water bodies	Filling in deeper parts with sediments; damming streams; modifying the shoreline by bulkheading, infilling, etc.; dredging to deepend parts of the basin; stirring up bottom by boating and shipping.
Introduction of non-native organisms	Intentional stocking of preferred organisms which may nevertheless become pests; accidental invasion via canals; accidental introduction via bilge water, private aquaria, angler's bait buckets, etc.

increase in the total biomass of living material, certainly not of the most preferred species.

Market and sport value per unit biomass is generally much lower with small mid-water fish species than with large bottom species, and processing costs are higher. Similarly, the aesthetic value to recreationists of the rooted plants nearshore is higher than a pea-soup-like mixture of suspended algae and pollutants.

The overall effect on fisheries is that nearshore labour-intensive specialised fisheries (sport and commercial) tend to disappear though highly mechanised capital-intensive offshore enterprises may persist, if the combined stresses do not become excessive and if the fish are not so contaminated as to become a health threat for those who would eat them. Yachtsmen may quickly sail from polluted marinas through the foul nearshore water to the attractive offshore waters. Beaches are posted as hazardous to human health.

The combined effect is one of debasement and destabilisation of the system of the natural environment and its renewable resources with respect to the features of greatest value to humans.

By the early 1970s, cases of EDS were apparent in some 40 bays, harbours, streams and estuaries in the Great Lakes. These eventually came to be termed "areas of concern". Many are severely contaminated. In the two lower Great Lakes, Erie and Ontario, the effects of the various areas of concern, each with a version of an EDS, ramified to the whole lake and influenced water quality and fisheries out to the deepest parts furthest from the shore. Furthermore, there are spillover effects from Lake Erie to Lake Ontario via the Niagara River and from Lake Ontario to the Gulf of St. Lawrence via the St. Lawrence River.

It is an intriguing prospect that the areas of concern - with their syndrome - may have some general systemic similarities with the degraded urban cores of some cities in the Great Lakes Basin, and perhaps with some degraded agricultural areas in parts of the Basin where the forest and agricultural resources had become abused and degraded. From an appropriate ecosystemic vantage point we may come to view such "areas of concern" - in the lakes, in the cities, on the land - as exhibiting some comparable features of an EDS.

Each involves:

- debasement of the higher qualities of the living system - both cultural and material - with a concomitant eruption of lower qualities;
- some general impoverishment in that the productive processes are impaired;
- destabilisation with consequent erratic swings in system properties;
- a kind of synergism of forces that contribute to the ecosystemic degradation syndrome which renders simple one-factor solutions impotent; and so on.

It may be that the consequences of conventional economic development in the Third World have also generated ecosystemic degradation syndromes with respect to aquatic, terrestrial and urban parts of regional ecosystems. If so, it may be time to banish CED from our Biosphere and foster instead new approaches that combine some successful traditional husbandry practices with new forms of intermediate technology all in the context of a sensitive appreciation for the ecosystemic problems and opportunities associated with a particular "bioregion" or regional man-nature ecosystem.

SOME PROBLEMS WITH REFORMS

The more southerly third of the Great Lakes Basin is the home of over 30 million humans. It is commercialised, industrialised, and urbanised. But the worst of the degradation of the Basin may be over. Corrective actions, mainly directed to point source pollution control have been implemented in recent decades and are beginning to have desirable ecosystemic consequences.

Some corrective programs have been undertaken at the binational level through formal conventions or agreements between Canada and the United States. One, begun in 1955, concerned control of an invading fish predator, the sea lamprey, that played a major role in destroying the most preferred fish species. Another agreement, of 1972, involved control of wastes that enrich water bodies especially with phosphorus, and cause eutrophication which in turn brings various undesirable consequences. The third, of 1978, concerns toxic contaminants. Some of the 1,000 or so chemicals which have been found in the aquatic ecosystem accumulate ecologically to toxic levels in fish and birds. They may then be transmitted to humans through ingestion of fish and through other ecological and epidemiological pathways. The first two of these agreements, of 1955 and 1972, have been quite successful with important though partial ecological recoveries that have spurred some cultural and economic redevelopments. Integrated management of the sea lamprey has so far cost over $100 million (1985 U.S. dollar equivalents) and control of nutrients has cost over $10 billion (in those units). The third, toxic contaminants, involves very complex phenomena that are not yet understood well enough to indicate just how those abuses can be corrected to a comparable degree; costs will likely exceed $10 billion (see units above).

Two other programs related to the Great Lakes Basin have been fostered very largely through less formal coordination at the level of the eight American states and one Canadian province within the Basin. These involve the introduction of desirable fish species - some salmonids - as a way of mitigating some of the consequences of the ecological degradation syndrome and as a way of enhancing the fishery resources. The overall costs of this mitigative/enhancement program may already have exceeded $100 million (see units above). The second concerns measures to correct and prevent a tendency to overfish the shared resources; this approach was accomplished in part by a re-allocation of fishery resources from hundreds of commercial fishermen with efficient capture methods to thousands of sport fishermen with very inefficient capture methods. The direct costs of this re-allocation relate mostly to administrative and court costs together with purchase of excess fishing capacity and likely did not exceed $50 million (see units above). The two programs - to introduce and foster large salmonids and to re-allocate resources to anglers - are interconnected politically.

Other threats are emerging or intensifying for the Great Lakes which may yet reverse some beginnings of the ecological recovery noted recently. Consumptive use of water is increasing with a threat of lowering of water levels and flows. This will likely have some undesirable ecological consequences and also exacerbate the adverse effects of some existing abuses. This threat is recognised primarily at the level of the Great Lakes States and Provinces.

The problems associated with long range transport of airborne pollutants - toxic fall-out and acid rain - are intensifying. This will need to be addressed by the two federal governments, perhaps in the context of a formal intergovernmental agreement at the level of the Northern Hemisphere, if not the Biosphere.

Meanwhile, with the "areas of concern", where the ecosystem degradation syndrome is still especially intense, the more local forms of government are likely to assert leadership. Responsibility for human health, and for certain land, water and waste management practices are regulated at that level. Municipalities and local planning and conservation authorities will need to become increasingly involved if remediation and rehabilitation of such areas of concern are to show progress.

Altogether the reforms of abuses of conventional exploitive development, as they affect the Great Lakes themselves, are coming to involve all levels of government. Some abuses can only be reversed by action at the highest level while others can be best reversed at the most local level. To orchestrate these initiatives in a multijurisdictional basin is an opportunity that now appears to be practicable. But the effort needed to succeed is immense.

CONCLUSION

It may be that our unfortunate experiences with conventional economic development, in the Great Lakes Basin and elsewhere in the over-developed and improperly-developed parts of the Western World, have parallels in the Third World. Of course, there may well be causal connections between them, as indicated in a "heartland-hinterland model" of the global economic system.

There seems little doubt that humanity cannot afford the long term cost and deleterious consequences of conventional economic development. It is time to try to learn from recent efforts to reform CED. These reforms may well not yet be sufficient in scope and depth to render our culture sustainable ecologically. What more needs to be done? As a research priority, this ranks exceptionally high.

REFERENCES

Carroll, J.E. (1983) *Environmental Diplomacy*: *An Examination and a Prospective of Canadian - United States Transboundary Environmental Relations*, Ann Arbor, Michigan: The University of Michigan Press, xxiii.

Francis, G.R., Magnuson, J.J., Regier, H.A. and Talhelm, D.R. (1979) *Rehabilitating Great Lakes Ecosystems*: *A Feasibility Study*, Ann Arbor, Michigan: Great Lakes Fishery Commission, Technical Report No. 37.

Francis, G.R., Grima, A.P., Regier, H.A. and Whillans, T.H. (1985) *A Prospectus for the Management of the Long Point System*, Ann Arbor, Michigan: Great Lakes Fishery Commission, Technical Report No. 43.

Harris, H.J., Talhelm, D.R., Magnuson, J.J. and Forbes, A.M. (1982) *Green Bay in the Future - A Rehabilitative Prospectus*, Ann Arbor, Michigan: Great Lakes Fishery Commission, Technical Report No. 38.

International Joint Commission (1982) *First Biennial Report Under the Great Lakes Water Quality Agreement of 1978*, Windsor, Ontario: Great Lakes Regional Office, iii.

International Joint Commission (1984) *Second Biennial Report under the Great Lakes Water Quality Agreement of 1978*, Windsor, Ontario: Great Lakes Regional Office, iii.

International Joint Commission (1985) *Report of the Great Lakes Science Advisory Board*, Windsor, Ontario: Great Lakes Regional Office.

International Joint Commission (1985) *Report of the Great Lakes Water Quality Board for 1984*, Windsor, Ontario: Great Lakes Regional Office.

Lee, B.J., Regier, H.A. and Rapport, D.J. (1982) "Ten ecosystem approaches to the planning and management of the Great Lakes," *Journal of Great Lakes Research*, 8: 505-19.

Malone, T.F. and Roedever, J.G. (1984) "Global change," *ICSU Press Symposium Series* No. 5.

Ontario Ministry of Natural Resources (1984) "Futures in water," *Proceedings of the Ontario Water Resources Conference*, June 12-14, Toronto, Ontario.

Rapport, D.J. and Regier, H.A. (1980) "An ecological approach to environmental information," *Ambio*, 9(1): 22-7.

Regier, H.A. and Baskerville, G.L. (1985) "Sustainable redevelopment of regional ecosystems degraded by exploitive development," in Clark, W.C. and Munn, R.E. (eds.), *Sustainable Development of the Biosphere*, Cambridge: Cambridge University Press (in press).

Regier, H.A. and Grima, A.P. (1984) "The nature of Great Lakes ecosystems as related to transboundary pollution," *International Business Lawyer*, June: 261-69.

Regier, H.A. and Grima, A.P. (1985) "On the allocation of fish to fishermen," *Canadian Journal of Fish and Aquatic Sciences*, 42: 845-59.

Segar, D.A. and Davis, P.G. (1984) *Contamination of Populated Estuaries and Adjacent Coastal Ocean - A Global Review*, Rockville, Maryland: U.S. Department of Commerce, National Oceanic and Atmospheric Agency, NOAA Tech. Memo. NOS OMA 11, vii.

CHAPTER 9

LAND USE AND/OR RESOURCE AND ENVIRONMENTAL INVENTORY CLASSIFICATION

CANADA CENTRE FOR REMOTE SENSING: INTERNATIONAL TECHNOLOGY TRANSFER ACTIVITY

Bill Bruce
and
Jean-Claude Henein
Canada Centre for Remote Sensing
Ottawa, Ontario

REMOTE SENSING FOR DEVELOPMENT

Nations of the developing world face an uncertain future dominated by grave and immediate economic and social problems. The wise development of natural resources in most cases provides the only real source of domestic support for growth and stability. Success in this basic national mission will be determined by the ability to implement a realistic and secure national resource development policy. Such a policy would be very difficult to implement without adequate timely information on the status of natural resources.

Unfortunately, developing nations share the common legacy of inadequate, often nonexistent resource information bases. The support of extensive data collection infrastructure is a luxury that can rarely be indulged. The sheer magnitude of the tasks, and the urgency, render conventional survey and data collection techniques inadequate.

There is, however, much recently justified optimism regarding the role of the so called "high" technologies such as remote sensing, in helping to resolve this problem. There is solid evidence that careful and appropriate application of remote sensing can aid vitally in the supply of basic resource information required for planned development.

To be broadly effective, the development and integration of remote sensing must be undertaken at the national level through the establishment of a coordinated national program. Such efforts are also necessary to make effective use of the usually scattered but vital donor agency project funds. The time is too short and the technology too complex to rely on scattered ad-hoc experimentation or trial and error approaches when it is operational use which is required.

The operational imperative should be built into all elements of the national program and of the development assistance strategies which support it from outside.

Tempering this optimism based on the capabilities of the "new" technologies, must be the realisation that access to technology is not universal and expertise in its application to the practical problems of development is not well advanced. Remote sensing can be a costly technology. Its development has until recently focused on technology "push", often to the benefit of the developers. These realities give little comfort to nations with pressing needs, that are competing for limited aid support in finance and expertise.

Planning of training activities must recognise not only the technologic potential of remote sensing, but also the infrastructure within which the newly required knowledge must be applied.

The success stories, and there are success stories, invariably come from nations which have organised themselves to apply a national perspective to the development and application of remote sensing appropriate to national development goals, priorities and supporting policies.

CANADA AND THE WORLD REMOTE SENSING COMMUNITY

By world standards, Canada has been involved in remote sensing a long time. A national remote sensing program was already being planned in 1969. In 1971 Canada became the first nation to establish a fully integrated national remote sensing program. The Canada Centre for Remote Sensing (CCRS) was created within the Federal Ministry of Energy, Mines and Resources as the executing agency.

With more than a decade of operational experience in all aspects of remote sensing, Canada has attracted much interest from nations with similar program objectives. Canada has become a recognised authority on adapting and applying remote sensing to meet demonstrated needs. In the process, we have become a significant force in the development of the technology. Canadian industrial partners have expanded from a modest domestic base to become world leaders in the manufacturing and support sectors. Canada is considering the option of joining the nations with remote sensing satellite capability with the launch of **RADARSAT** at the end of this decade.

Our country has persisted in this technology because continuing development hinges on our ability to obtain accurate and timely information for managing Canadian natural resources. As a major user of remote sensing, and a developer of the technology, Canada is thus keenly, perhaps uniquely, aware of the challenges facing developing nations. A developing nation in many respects itself, Canada can work with Third World nations to provide advice and support as requested, to ensure that the interests of users everywhere are represented.

CANADIAN DEVELOPMENT ASSISTANCE ACTIVITIES

CCRS participation in development assistance has taken many forms. This is done through those Canadian government agencies with international development responsibilities: The Canadian International Development Agency (CIDA) and the International Development Research Centre (IDRC). This ensures that the Canadian development assistance effort is properly coordinated and is consistent with Canadian foreign policy.

The three projects outlined below serve to illustrate remote sensing technology transfer in widely different geographic settings and development contexts.

Project "PERCEP"

Project "PERCEP" involved Canada and Peru from 1976 to 1981. The technology transfer project design was based on the concept of shared responsibility through joint project management. The cornerstones to its success have been close, continuous communication at the management level and broad exposure of Peruvian experts to operational remote sensing through on-the-job training with Canadian counterparts at CCRS. These factors have ensured continuity of Peruvian involvement and support.

Although modest in funding, the CIDA sponsored project provided 60 man-months of intensive research and training experiences to the Peruvian Remote Sensing Team. A complete remote sensing applications facility, based on a jointly developed design, has been outfitted during the project. In addition, a remote sensing library was set up and an English-Spanish Remote Sensing Glossary prepared in Peru under project sponsorship. There is already ample evidence that many Peruvian specialists and resource programs have benefited from the project and are using remote sensing routinely. Continuity of personnel on the job after training is a factor which is considered critical for successful technology transfer. In spite of difficult economic conditions, the majority of the Peruvian specialists who received training during the project continue to apply remote sensing in their day-to-day work. Several project team members have been promoted to positions of increased responsibility in their organisations. At an institution level, the use of remote sensing has intensified and expanded. Locally organised and supported courses and workshops continue on a regular basis, and interest is active in further expanding Peruvian remote sensing activities. Following an intensive project evaluation, CIDA has agreed to sponsor a second phase of this project to broaden Peruvian remote sensing capabilities. A national remote sensing organisation has been established in Peru and other donor nations have since offered additional support. The new project should begin later in 1985.

West Africa

The second major international program undertaken by CCRS under CIDA sponsorship involves the countries of the Sahel region in West Africa. In this project Canadian efforts, through CCRS, were concentrated initially in the areas of coordination, training and applications development.

This project was part of an international effort involving the United States, France and Canada. Canada assisted in establishing a regional training centre in Ouagadougou, Upper Volta, and provided the full time services of a Deputy Director to assist the African Director of the Centre. Several development projects were sponsored by CIDA and IDRC, in the critical fields of hydrology, forestry and agrometeorology. The activities of the regional remote sensing centre focused on training of African counterparts from each of the participating nations. The project concentrated on the problems of establishing and demonstrating remote sensing technology at a regional level. In spite of the obvious difficulties in doing so, it is now recognised that greater acceptance and momentum could have been established if the substantial regional training efforts had been more adequately supported by country-level efforts to ensure that basic physical and administrative infrastructure existed in each country.

Thailand

Thailand has long been involved in remote sensing and recently established a domestic Landsat satellite receiving and processing capability. On the strength of established bilateral linkages in remote sensing, CCRS offered to provide training/research support to the National Council of Thailand and other agencies involved in remote sensing. Much of the Thai equipment was similar to that operated by CCRS, thus increasing the potential relevance of any training activities undertaken. Under this industry cooperation agreement CCRS provided long term training to six Thai specialists.

Based on the highly satisfactory results of this initial cooperation, CCRS has participated in a subsequent CIDA - funded remote sensing transfer program for Thai geologists.

Cooperation between the Canadian and Thai remote sensing programs has been very fruitful to date. This cooperation now seems likely to continue with CIDA's decision to fund a major applications development and technology transfer project to complement the program of infrastructure development already in place. CCRS has actively supported these initiatives.

The design of the new project recognises the growing Thai expertise in remote sensing by focusing on domestic and on-site training and project development activities. The movement toward greater sharing of project design and management decision making proved a timely and sound one in the case of the previous project and is being pursued for future cooperative remote sensing activities between Canada and Thailand.

CONCLUSIONS

What began as largely piecemeal responses to requests has evolved with experience into a conceptual model which emphasises broad technology transfer objectives for such activities. This model recognises the need for flexibility of response while recognising the constraints within which these activities must be carried out.

Perhaps because our partners and ourselves knew we were breaking new ground, our approach remained flexible. This proved to be an important and positive element in the assistance model.

In basic terms the model stresses comprehensive and appropriate technology transfer through shared management responsibility. It requires that a close partnership be established between CCRS and its counterpart organisation in the recipient country. The task of technology transfer is defined broadly, recognising the following seven elements:

- access to technology
- knowledge
- experience
- facilities
- management
- mandate
- policy.

It is evident that these elements imply a variety of training and local research needs. The various training components can be made more practically effective if they are seen as part of a technology transfer and local technology generation plan which is based on a realistic assessment of practical needs and individual capabilities.

Individual programs are designed so that to the extent possible, all of the above elements are either addressed in training or research activities or at least formally recognised by all parties. It should be evident that a conscious and flexible application of this concept model can, and has, led to the design, implementation, and management of successful technology transfer under widely varying conditions.

The importance of remote sensing as an appropriate technology for developing nations is now becoming widely acknowledged. Canadian experience in international remote sensing technology transfer has been very rewarding. There is growing recognition, fueled by recent positive experience that development assistance activities aimed at the transfer of remote sensing technology can, if properly designed, result in a positive and mutually beneficial experience.

Domestic capabilities and needs vary widely among developing nations. CCRS experience has demonstrated that effective technology transfer is possible under widely differing conditions as illustrated by examples from Latin America, West Africa and Southeast Asia. Success depends on the application of a flexible conceptual model which recognises domestic capabilities and development objectives. Close conscious coordination of infrastructure support and training components of such remote sensing projects is critical for long term success in technology transfer.

A RECOMMENDATION REGARDING THE ESTABLISHMENT OF REMOTE SENSING TECHNOLOGY IN THIRD WORLD COUNTRIES

Simsek Pala
Ontario Centre for Remote Sensing
Toronto, Ontario

THE POTENTIAL OF SATELLITE REMOTE SENSING FOR THIRD WORLD COUNTRIES

Satellite remote sensing of earth resources has been marked by very rapid technological development over the past decade. Impressive progress has also been made in the technology of digital image processing and analysis; however, this technology still lags behind the technology of data recording and transmission. Not only have there been major improvements in data resolution and volume, but also a steady increase in the number of satellites carrying remote sensors. Furthermore, construction of the United States space station is now scheduled to begin in the 1990s - a development which will have a profound impact on remote sensing. The future remote sensing data supply may thus be fundamentally secure.

In many application areas, it has been demonstrated that satellite data analysis, together with the production of hard-copy maps of the results, provides an effective, rapid and economic method for natural resource inventory and environmental monitoring.

For vast areas of the earth, in developed as well as Third World countries, no adequate information exists on natural resources - information essential to effective decision making and planning. If properly analysed, satellite data can yield much of this information. For example, in the province of Ontario, Canada, the Ontario Centre for Remote Sensing has developed applications of satellite data analysis and computerised thematic map production which provide regional information on land cover, forest resources, agricultural land use, wetlands and peat resources.

Two fundamental factors are involved in the success of any remote sensing program, particularly in the Third World: the expertise of the project contractor(s) and the appropriateness' of the aid program to technological conditions in the receiving country.

REMOTE SENSING EXPERTISE OF CONTRACTOR FROM DONOR COUNTRY

It would seem self-evident that any contractor undertaking a remote sensing development project as a part of a Third World aid program must be thoroughly knowledgeable and experienced in the practical employment of this new technology. If the contractor is not competent enough, its efforts will do more harm than good, by forming the basis of mistaken action and by discrediting the technology itself.

Over the past ten years, educational institutions, both universities and technical colleges, have developed a selection of individual courses in response to the need to impart remote sensing skills to young professionals. In Canada, at least, this process has been less than systematic and has been seriously restricted, in the areas of digital image analysis in particular, by a lack of funds for equipment; nevertheless, the initiatives of certain individual institutions have been both energetic and successful. Opportunities do exist for students at the university level to gain a basis in remote sensing fundamentals and some limited exposure to application.

Professionals already working in a natural resource or engineering field do not have the same opportunities; therefore, although they bring invaluable disciplinary experience to the performance of a Third World remote sensing project, they are often in need of special intensive training in remote sensing.

The necessary background in sensors and recording systems may be presented effectively in the form of a training course. The principles of visual and digital image analysis may also be covered. However, the most effective way for a working professional to develop expertise in the use of satellite remote sensing is to collaborate with an experienced remote sensing specialist in performing a demonstration project.

ADAPTATION OF REMOTE SENSING AID TO THIRD WORLD CONDITIONS

For the purposes of distributing aid effectively, it is useful to group Third World countries into two general categories on the basis of their level of technological advancement.

One group consists of countries where virtually no professional or technical infrastructure exists on which remote sensing expertise could be developed. In these countries, it may be extremely difficult to keep a computer installation dust-free and cool or to have simple maintenance done consistently over a period of years. There is no point in providing aid in the form of hardware under these circumstances. Even if the scientists of these countries were well trained abroad and possessed great enthusiasm and personal aptitude, the structure of the government and economy might prevent them from continuing their work after the foreign funding had been withdrawn. The donor country would thus be obliged to run the operation on a permanent basis. Setting political considerations aside, this is an impractical and wasteful form of aid, as it achieves no real internal development.

In such cases, it would be more effective for IDRC to "assign" a Canadian university or company to a specific country or countries, and to purchase the necessary hardware for that university or company. The hardware would be used in training the scientists from abroad and collaborating with them on research and development and operational projects in Canada. The advantages of such a form of aid are as follows:

1. A large number of professionals and technicians, from several different countries, could be trained at the same time.
2. They would gain experience from collaboration on projects performed to operational standards.
3. Information useful to the developing country would be produced.
4. The trainees would be exposed to the day-to-day process of project management.
5. Only one set of equipment would be needed to provide aid to several countries.
6. The equipment would be maintained and operated properly.
7. The Canadian university or company would gain a high-technology facility difficult to obtain in any other way, as well as extremely valuable operational experience.

In short, IDRC would achieve more with less money.

Canadian know-how in remote sensing hardware and software production, as well as application and training, is recognised as among the best in the world. It makes far more sense to bring the trainees to the source than to try to duplicate Canadian conditions at an early stage in a developing country.

The second group is made up of countries where remote sensing is practised to some extent, but where the most advanced technology has not yet been introduced. In these circumstances, aid in the form of equipment is effective, when combined with collaboration on research and application projects with scientists from the receiving country. This kind of collaboration requires that the selected donor agency devote itself to trainees from one country at a time. The projects can be carried out either in the donor country or the receiving country, depending on the facilities available at the time.

CONCLUSION

If current plans come to fruition, the number of earth-resource satellite systems in operation will increase significantly over the next ten years. As developing countries have the greatest gap to fill in natural resources information, they will have the most to gain from the new wealth of data. With its international remote sensing development program, therefore, IDRC is making a far-sighted contribution to the future development of these countries. But it is also providing an important stimulus to the advancement of remote sensing expertise in Canada.

GEOGRAPHIC INFORMATION SYSTEMS TECHNOLOGY FOR ENVIRONMENTAL RESOURCE MANAGEMENT IN THE THIRD WORLD

Ian K. Crain
and
Jean Thie
Lands Directorate, Environment Canada
Ottawa, Ontario

GEOGRAPHIC INFORMATION SYSTEMS

The term "geographic information system" or GIS is very broad and encompasses all systems designed to store and manipulate data which relate to locations on the earth's surface. Common applications are land and resource inventories, the census, urban planning, etc. where the data banks will contain locational references such as a county, or the actual boundaries of land parcels. Other equivalent terms for such information are "spatial" and "geo-coded" data. Because of the need to manipulate extremely large quantities of data, most modern GIS employ computer technology, although many earlier systems used manual techniques.

A GIS must handle two distinctive types of date - *graphical data*, consisting of the geometric entities of points, lines and areas, and *attribute data*, the nongeographical items which describe the geometric entities. For example, an artesian well might have its latitude/longitude location (*graphical* data) along with the well type, water chemistry, depth, etc. (*attribute* data).

Typically, a GIS will have three components:

1. **Input and editing**
2. **Data manipulation**
3. **Output and display.**

Input and editing consists of the collection of data from multiple sources, such as aerial photography, satellite imagery, maps and statistical reports, its review and correction and its transformation into a consistent format suitable for future use, thus creating a data base. In order for graphical data such as lines and areas to be machine-readable, they must be transformed into a series of point locations represented numerically in some consistent coordinate system. This process is referred to as "digitising" and is performed using specialised equipment such as large tablets on which an operator traces lines with an electronic cursor, or by optically scanning a map.

Manipulation of the attribute data is done in the same way as any conventional data processing system; however, the manipulation of graphical data requires complex mathematical processing. Typical graphical manipulations allow for the changing of map projection, contouring of point data, determining the intersections of overlapping polygons, data selection and generalisation, registering and superimposing various data sets, and a whole range of statistical analyses.

Data output and display consists of printed statistical reports and tabulations in response to user requests, as well as graphs and maps.

POTENTIAL APPLICATION OF GIS IN DEVELOPING COUNTRIES

The most valuable function of a GIS in a developing nation is *spatial data integration* - the bringing together of disparate resource and economic data sets to provide for a regional or national overview. Many Third World countries have completed various types of resource inventories covering large regions, often on a sectoral basis - forestry, agriculture, mineral resources, etc. A GIS is useful in such an exercise, and such inventories are of enormous importance as sources of baseline data. The inventories only begin to serve a productive role, however, when they can be integrated and then analysed to contribute to decisions leading to wise *management* of the environmental resources. It is in this role that the GIS excels and is thus of fundamental importance to achieving good resource planning and management (Thie *et al.*, 1982).

The steps required in such data integrations are:

- identifying and selecting appropriate data sources (often in map form);

- compiling or transferring the data to a consistent geographic reference base;
- combining and "overlaying" the various data sets to form an integrated spatial information base.

The second primary function of a GIS is data *analysis*. The analysis function includes:

- determining interrelationships between various data coverage;
- summarising and extracting critical variables from complex data;
- developing and determining suitability ratings, sensitivity measures and other indices;
- statistical analysis and summarisation in tabular and graphical form, suitable for policy makers.

These two primary functions are of particular benefit in interdisciplinary resource policy development activities in developing countries - such as analysing development conflicts between forestry, agriculture and urban growth, sectoral renewable and nonrenewable resource development planning, and the complexity of ensuring economic development in harmony with the natural and human environment. These and other resource management results are the primary outputs of the application of this technology (Crain and MacDonald, 1985).

The described GIS functions can be done manually with trained but not necessarily "high-technology" staff, and such manpower resources are commonly assumed to be readily available in developing countries. On the other hand, computer-based techniques provide a vital element of time reductions which is essential to making policy and planning decisions in step with resource development and population demand, and the quick response necessary for emergency assessments such as extensive famine, forest fires and flooding. Best use is made of the high technology GIS in its integration and analysis role, while applying more human-resource intensive technology to base-line data collection and first level interpretation.

CANADA'S ROLE IN GEOGRAPHIC INFORMATION SYSTEMS

Canada has the reputation as the "birthplace of GIS". The world's first operational GIS, the Canada Geographic Information System, was developed in Ottawa for the ARDA project, more than 20 years ago (Tomlinson *et al.*, 1976). The main thrust of that project was to develop a land capability classification system and compile an inventory of all the potentially productive land of Canada. The result was the Canada Land Inventory, (CLI), one of the most comprehensive and ambitious national surveys ever attempted. Early in the project it became clear that the volume of data to be analysed precluded manual methods and thus computer-based solutions were sought. The result was the creation of the CGIS, which in highly modified form, still operates today as a significant component of the Canada Land Data System (CLDS). Because of this pioneering work, a large number of the concepts, algorithms and terminology associated with today's geographic information systems are derived from the original CGIS. The generalised nature and design foresight of this early system have successfully allowed it to prosper under the direction of a number of different agencies and ministries over the years, and to improve and evolve continually to meet a broad range of data analysis and resource management applications well beyond the original expectations.

A number of key "firsts" were established at CGIS/CLDS. When the CGIS became fully implemented in 1971, it was the first general purpose GIS to go into production operation. It was the first system (and for many years the only system) to use raster scanning for efficient high volume input of manuscript maps. This required the custom design and construction (by IBM) of a large format optical drum scanner. Delivered in 1967, this device was only superceded in 1984 by a modern computer controlled scanner, a tribute to good design and robust construction.

Other firsts include, the employment of the now standard data structure of line segments or "arcs" chained together to form polygons, the principles of data compaction of linework now know as "Freeman encoding", the cellular graphic storage principal known as the "Morton Matrix", compact geo-coding to allow complete absolute geographic referencing of all data, the use of a hybrid raster-vector format for data representation, and the provision of remote interactive cartographic retrieval in a national network. Recent innovations include micro-computers for land data analysis and graphic input, and state-of-the-art multiprocessor hardware employing artificial intelligence techniques for interactive editing of input documents.

The client base for the CLDS now includes all of the primary land conservation programs of the Lands Directorate (National land use monitoring, ecological land surveys, federal land impact, acid rain sensitivity, arctic land planning, etc.) as well as other programs of Environment Canada, such as the National Parks Service, other federal government departments, such as Agriculture and Energy Mines and Resources, provincial governments and agencies, crown corporations, utilities, nonprofit environmental groups, and some private companies, and recently, multilateral organisations in aid of the Third World.

Other early systems in Canada include the Geographically Referenced Data Retrieval System of Statistics Canada started around 1965 and the Canada Soil Information System of Agriculture Canada. This pioneering work has continued and Canadian industry, universities and government laboratories are at the forefront of research and technology. For this reason they are looked to by multilateral agencies and Third World Countries for technology transfer in this field. The CLDS, for example, hosted 18 tours of visiting foreign technical experts in 1984.

RECENT EXPERIENCE IN GIS TECHNOLOGY TRANSFER

In the past year, the Lands Directorate has been involved in two experiences of technology transfer related to Environmental Resource Management in the Third World, one bi-lateral with Indonesia, and one multi-lateral with FAO. Brief descriptions of these activities follow:

Pilot Studies for FAO

A series of pilot or demonstration studies were performed with FAO staff using the CLDS facilities in the Autumn of 1984. The aim was to test the application of GIS techniques to FAO's mandate to collect and analyse data on land resources to find solutions to malnutrition, and land degradation in developing countries.

The study area chosen comprised 14 countries of West Africa. Some 11 thematic map coverages were available (with varying degrees of accuracy) for the region including soil, ecoclimatic zones, vegetation, watersheds, population, density, etc.

The objectives of the project were:

- To demonstrate the utility and effectiveness on CIS for FAO for storing, handling and analysing geographic information in support of major programs by:
  - demonstrating the analytical effectiveness of a GIS to deal with specific disciplinary and inter-disciplinary questions;
  - demonstrating the feasibility of integrating the data bases from different resource sectors.

- To assess the user friendliness of the GIS system.
- To develop expertise on GIS in FAO.
- To evaluate the cost in relation to the benefits.
- To assess the resources, manpower and system configuration needed for a GIS in FAO.

The approach taken was to perform a series of well defined "exercises", which were essentially environmental questions for which answers were sought. This led to applying the appropriate geographic manipulation, analysis facilities and models to obtain the desired outputs. One example was to determine the fuel wood production capacity by ecoclimatic zone compared to the fuel wood requirements of the population. Other exercises involved food self-sufficiency, livestock overstocking rates, etc.

The highly positive result of these studies has encouraged FAO to proceed with the development of their own capability which has to date included the transfer of the geographic data analysis software of CLDS to the FAO computer centre in Rome.

Geographic Information Systems in Indonesia

The general status in Indonesia with respect to the need for Environmental Information Systems was well expressed by Hainsworth (1985) as follows:

An enormous difficulty for environmentalists in seeking to advance their perspective (in competition, for example, with hard-line economists) is lack of data. Quantitative information on environmental depletion, regeneration and potential for Indonesia is almost nonexistent. What sometimes appear as "environmental statistics" are mostly sectoral output data or budgetary outlays for sectoral programs. Reasonably current information that does come available circulates mostly by word of mouth and cannot readily be verified. Much of it is anecdotal or very localised, and it tests credibility to generalise at the national level from such an information base. This poses real obstacles to any attempt to provide an objective assessment on the State of the Environment.

A senior member of the Lands Directorate was invited to join a project team of the Environmental Manpower Development in Indonesia Project of the Institute of Resource and Environmental Studies of Dalhousie University, with the objective of advising on information system development needs in Indonesia.

The particular client for the advice was the Ministry of State for Population and the Environment (KLH) who categorised their requirements as:

- generalised integrated environmental information for purposes of national policy making. Clients for this information are the Minister of KLH, other senior cabinet members and the President;
- integrated environmental information for the academic and research community, especially, work-in-progress information so as to avoid duplication and provide more effective and more efficient research;
- summarised and digested information for NGO's, the Press, and thereby, Indonesian society in general.

Three general classes of information were seen as needed:

- National and regional environmental indicators to provide for "State of the Environment" reporting and the monitoring and analysis of environmental issues, especially as they relate to population, e.g. agriculture/forestry interface, population/agriculture interface, transmigration, water quality, etc.
- More focussed base-line and issue-response information for generalised environmental impact assessment, especially of proposed government policies and actions.
- Early warning information on environmental emergencies such as: volcanic eruptions, forest fires, oil spills, etc. Emphasis here was on ensuring the rapid flow and dissemination of relevant data which exists on a sectoral basis.

On the other hand, it was clear that large quantities of relevant environmental information exist in Indonesia in various sectors. The overwhelming need is for facilities to integrate, analyse and generalise quickly the data for purposes of national policy setting.

Among the recommendations from this study are:

- that KLH should build on the single existing GIS in their mapping agency;
- that KLH should seek to develop expertise through the secondment of technical personnel to operational GIS systems in Canada.

The potential advantages of the introduction of GIS Technology for national scale data integration in Indonesia are significant and the timing apparently ripe. The particular advantages would be for national level resource assessment which would enable the rational and systematic development of national environmental policies and guidelines, and the provision of means to monitor the impact of such policies after implementation. The next few years will indicate whether this potential can be realised.

CONCLUDING REMARKS

Canadian GIS technology has enormous potential and in some cases proven beneficial to the Third World to assist in environmental resource management. An important lesson from the two case studies presented here is that success in the application of GIS technology for resource management comes from clearly defining the problem, expressing it in modelling terms and *then* applying the GIS to integrate the data from existing inventories into the format needed for the model. It was demonstrated that in relatively short time periods (a few weeks) the integration of continental scale data sets (some quite poor) can be achieved and useful generalised indicators produced. Both the quickness and the ability to make the best of poor or incomplete data are important factors for practical application in the Third World.

REFERENCES

Crain, I.K. and MacDonald, C.L. (1985) "From land inventory to land management - the evolution of a geographic information system," *Cartographica*, 21(2-3): 40-6.

Hainsworth, G. (1985) "Economic growth, basic needs and environment in Indonesia - the search for harmonious development," *Southeast Asian Affairs*, pp. 152-76.

Thie, J., Switzer, W.A. and Chartrand, N. (1982) "Das Canada Land Data System und seine Anwendungsmoglichkeiten in Landschaftsplanning and Bewirtschaftung der Ressourcen," *Natur und Landschaft*, 57(12): 433-40 (English translation available in CLDS Internal Report, R001071).

Tomlinson, R.F., Calkins, H.W. and Markle, D.F. (1976) "The Canada geographic information system," Ch. 4, in *Computer Handling of Geographical Data*, Paris: The UNESCO Press, pp. 27-73.

CHAPTER 10

IMPACT EVALUATION STUDIES, PLANNING, AND MANAGEMENT

COST-EFFECTIVENESS OF ENVIRONMENTAL MANAGEMENT IN THE CONTEXT OF THIRD WORLD DEVELOPMENT

Robert S. Dorney
School of Urban and Regional Planning
University of Waterloo
and
Ecoplans Limited
Waterloo, Ontario

INTRODUCTION

The perception of business and political leaders in many countries is that the environmental movement of the 1970s resulted in higher costs for development, with uncertain economic benefits, if any. Thus many Third World countries attending the Stockholm Conference suggested that environmental management was a "frill" which only wealthy nations could afford; this perception in part still exists. This perception can also be found in business leaders and in politicians in Canada as well, as the recent publication by Loucks, Perkowski and Bowie (1982) demonstrates for the energy industry, in spite of other earlier and more recent data which shows substantial benefits over costs for a wide range of development projects (Dorney, 1973).

This paper, then, will explore the issues of costs and benefits in terms of economics, not intangible benefits. It is based on consulting experience in North America, Central and South America, as well as the Middle East. In addition to an assignment with the UNDP, I was program specialist with the OAS (1963-1967) in the resource management field, and spent two sabbaticals in Turkey and Costa Rica.

THE PROFESSIONAL SCOPE OF ENVIRONMENTAL MANAGEMENT

Although the field of environmental management (EM) is still evolving, enough practical experience has been gained that a definition can be attempted. EM then is a systems oriented profession, it is interdisciplinary, and it integrates the engineering, natural and social sciences in the context of design, production, diversity, stability, rehabilitation and reclamation, and the self-organising properties of human and natural landscapes at both the urban and regional scale. From this perspective it deals with the environment from both a structural and process point of view. As currently practiced, it has two distinct phases - an environmental or ecoplanning phase, and an environmental protection phase - a "paper game" and a "hard hat game" (Figure 1). The flow in this figure is left to right; the black dots represent EM interventions. Four modes are shown; these modes are distinct in an operational sense, but of course, policy formulation impinges on the others to a great extent.

In Canada, the practitioners of EM have been drawn from the ranks of other fields, principally from geography, natural sciences, physical planning, landscape architecture, and systems/civil engineering, plus law, in that order. In Ontario, the Ontario Society of Environmental Management, formed in 1977, has developed minimum standards and a code of ethics to assist in professional identification and development. Most of its 75 members also hold membership in other Learned Societies or Professions, such as the Canadian Institute of Planners. In the United States, the National Association of Environmental Professionals is an independent effort. This university is one of the few which teaches courses in the professional practice of EM.

Currently, with an estimated 150-200 full time professionals practicing or teaching EM in Ontario, the field is small compared with civil engineering (7,000);[1] architecture (1,600), planning (862), or forestry (686); it is similar in size to landscape architecture (200).

The economic impetus for EM professionals developed from the field of impact assessment. Although the level of impact assessment varies depending on the vigour in the economy, current estimates for Ontario are in the vicinity of $10,000,000 on construction costs about 1,000 times higher. Based on this level of professional activity,

----

[1] Professional numbers are based on 1977 Statistics Canada data plus phone calls to some of the Associations.

ENVIRONMENTAL PLANNING OR ECOPLANNING PHASE | ENVIRONMENTAL PROTECTION PHASE

Mode	Organization and Administration Stage	Analytical Stage	Evaluation and Design Stage	Report Stage	Hearings and Approvals Stage	Contract Stage	Construction Stage (As Part of Facility Development Mode)	Report Stage	Abatement and Enforcement Stage (As Part of Urban & Regional Operation Mode)	Rehabilitation Stage	Monitoring Stage	Research Stage
URBAN AND REGIONAL DEVELOPMENT MODE	●	●	●	●	●			●		As Needed	As Needed	As Needed
URBAN AND REGIONAL OPERATION MODE	●	●		●	As Needed			●	●	As Needed	●	●
POLICY FORMULATION MODE	●	●	●	●	●							As Needed
FACILITY DEVELOPMENT MODE	●	●	●	●	●	●	●	●	●	●	●	As Needed
FACILITY OR CORPORATE OPERATION MODE	●	●	●	●	As Needed				●	As Needed	●	As Needed
FACILITY DECOMMISSIONING MODE	●	●	●	●	●	●	●	●	●	●	●	●

The black dots indicate professional activity areas where environmental intervention is useful. The planning and protection sequences flow from left to right. The bottom two modes, facility or corporate operation mode, and facility decommissioning mode are not discussed in this paper. Because of severe penalties arising from insurance claims relating to the operation of the chemical industry and some mining industries (such as asbestos) environmental management procedures are expected to be increased, but the extent of the increase is still speculative; similarly, the cost-effectiveness of this intervention is unknown but will be offset against increased insurance costs, and decreased stock values for those companies operating in an unsafe manner.

Figure 1: The Environmental Management Process Broken into Two Phases - Planning and Protection

although not high in comparison to other levels of professional activity, the next question arises - is EM cost-effective?

THE ECONOMIC CONTEXT OF ENVIRONMENTAL MANAGEMENT

Using Figure 1, the economic dynamics of the four modes will be examined in turn from both a Canadian and a Third World perspective. Where information is spotty, research needs will be discussed. Since EM uses a "human ecology" construct, the regional sensitivity and the cultural sensitivity of EM will become evident.

Urban and Regional Development Mode

Since cities are extremely expensive to build, to operate, and to maintain, it might be expected that extensive comparative studies would be available in regards to the economics of EM. Such parameters as material flow systems and energy flow systems are straightforward accounting issues, but government statistics are not presently available at this level of detail in Canada; Japan is one of the few countries attempting to quantify some of these parameters. Fragmented information on the biological dynamics of urban ecosystems is available in Ontario (Dorney and McLellan, 1984); it demonstrates the costs of present biological activities, and the substantial economic advantages in moving derelict lands into agricultural production. For example, the City of Waterloo has 9 per cent of its 15,011 acres in abandoned agricultural land - or about 1,350 acres; market gardening of this acreage would generate cash flows into the million dollar range. By taking a holistic look at the biological systems of cities then, considerable savings in management costs appear to be possible; similar mapping of Escazu in Costa Rica demonstrated the high production of market gardens and fruit trees within the "quadras" and on the periphery of the village.

Considerations of in-city agricultural development appears then to offer some promise, especially where tropical fruit trees can be grown on small acreage. The anthropological dimension of this has been recently examined for Tikal in Guatemala (Flannery, 1982), where calculations demonstrate that this city of 80,000 was self-sufficient in terms of calorie flow within the city limits. If true, and this can be experimentally verified, agricultural development can benefit by introducing the historic-anthropological urban aspect into its traditional regional focus.

Turning to a regional development focus, in the early 1960s, Dr. W. Drewes, a geographer with the organisation of the American States, Washington, D.C., and I were asked to advise the Inter American Bank on the environmental aspects of the Rio de la Plata Project. Data were completely lacking on climatology, hydrology, soils, forestry, nature reserves, and fisheries; any prediction of impacts, positive or negative were impossible. Even the optimisation of energy production could not be done without climatological and hyrological data. The river basin development project as conceived was an ad-hoc planning process, politically driven. I believe it is reasonable to conclude that with some biophysical and cultural data, considerably more benefits could be derived from the projected investment of about one billion dollars US (1964 dollars). Proof that this investment was not an optimal one, of course, is not possible; but the question could be asked in this way - would you invest your personal dollars, pesos or whatever currency in the project? If you answer yes, I have all kinds of deals for you!

The Rio de la Plata project demonstrates the value of having regional data banks in place for abiotic, biotic and cultural resources (ABC data banks). Ontario Hydro has such a data bank for much of Ontario; it was compiled by consultants; it is operated by a staff of about ten. The cost of setting up such a data bank will vary, but its value in regional development and in facility development, such as transmission lines, lies in its ability to answer policy questions quickly, and with some lead time (6-12 months) allow for sophisticated impact analysis (whose cost-effectiveness is described later).

The economic value of EM in terms of environmental design for educational campuses, new towns, and subdivisions can be found in Dorney (1973, 1977a, 1986). The savings generally are high in the geotechnical-geomorphology-economic mineral side of EM; over the years such issues as slope stability, shale warping, karst topography, marine clays, natural gas leakage in shales, gypsum have been uncovered by adequate biophysical analysis in the framework of EM and urban design. The potential damage to property and the potential loss in human life have been obvious enough to have resulted in redesign of the project in some cases. Tens of thousands invested in geological sciences can save millions of dollars with a high frequency (about 20 per cent of the time in approximately 50 projects). Other savings arise from protection of urban trees; $20 spent in a tree by tree inventory system can generate increased lot values on the order of $1,000 to $5,000 per lot; for details, see Dorney, Evered and Kitchen (1986). Amenity values through open space analysis were shown to increase net profit per acre from $10,295 to $15,924 in one comparative study in Waterloo; the approximate cost to undertake EM for urban development is on the order of 0.6 per cent of the value of a lot ready for sale to a builder. Taken as a whole then, I have found EM as a fundamental building block for appropriate urban design. I believe it demonstrates, that a single discipline simply cannot develop the sophisticated fit between man and nature that a multidiscipline based on study can provide; front end costs are marginally higher, but the substantial advantages in a geological-biological-amenity package are high; these advantages can result in more profit to the developer, less expensive housing for the consumer or both.

Urban and Regional Government Operation Mode

Cost-effectiveness information for this mode seems to be deficient. Governments do not undertake these kind of "internal audits" except, of course, in a more political-priorities context. Programs are added due to internal or external pressures, and just as easily deleted for the same reasons. However, by looking at the level of expenditures in 20 countries in this hemisphere, based on 1965 OAS data and 1977 Canadian data, expenditures in all the resource management agencies falls in the range of 0 to 3 per cent (Dorney, unpublished OAS data for the Mar del Plata Conference on Renewable Natural Resources, and Dorney, 1977b). EM would hence be a fraction of this small percentage. Given the dependence of man on clean and abundant or adequate water resources, on sufficient soil of high productivity, on sufficient fibre for paper and chemicals as well as heat and construction, such mineral expenditures do not suggest an impending crisis. Compared to military expenditures EM then is essentially invisible; yet, it is only through resources management and EM (the next level of integration) that long term survival of a culture becomes likely. It would be productive then, to examine the question of what level of EM is cost-effective in the context of national survival. A pragmatic reading of history of much of the Middle East and northern Africa attests to the civilizations which could raise armies and which could build monuments, but could not manage their landscape resources to maintain long term biological productivity. For much of the world then, EM offers promise in the rehabilitation of derelict landscapes, as well as for the conservation of productivity.

On a slightly different vein, in Canada the energy industry in cooperation with the National Energy Board examined the issue of "overregulation". The results (NEB, 1984) make interesting reading. Although costs of regulation are significant, on one large pipeline project $83,000,000 was saved by recalculating the need for the proposed size of the gas pipeline; apparently the company had made some miscalculations on the proposed $522,000,000 project. How many other "errors" have slipped through in the past because of "underregulation".

Urban and Regional Policy Formulation Mode

Because of time lags between policy formulation and implementation, not to mention monitoring for effectiveness, any cost-effectiveness information is difficult to obtain. Likely the results would not be useful to other regions or situations. Perhaps the best we can expect then is to suggest that continued policy research on various aspects of environmental quality would be useful.

As an example, I have been associated with a Master's thesis on the effectiveness of the Foodland Guidelines in Ontario, a policy to protect blocks of agricultural land from urban encroachment. It appears that the policy has been effective (LeBlanc, 1983). Essentially what this means is that money which would have flowed somewhat loosely into the countryside was diverted or lost; its spending would have been encouraged in many municipalities hence may have gone into the urban zone. Net benefits are not available, but the social benefits derived from the protection of farmland are sufficient to continue the policy into the second decade.

Similarly, the Waterloo Regional Official Policies Plan[2] protected the high capability farmland from urbanisation. If agriculture is forced onto less productive land, the economic penalties are severe, in the order of 20-30 per cent increased production costs for the same yield. Thus the protection of farmland, utilising the land capability classification system, is justified on economic as well as on social grounds. An additional benefit in this Region is the survival of the old-order Mennonite way of life; this was made possible through policy dialogue at the time the Official Plan was prepared. To utilise their horse-powered technology special road standards were needed. Ten years later, we have achieved a mixed farming technology, where you can see horse-power being used next to $50,000 tractors in adjoining fields. The cost was approximately $250,000 for the

----

[2] Now under review after 10 years in operation.

overpass on Highway 86, $100,000 for the culvert under the freeway at St. Jacobs, and the continued operation of the bridge at St. Jacobs. With a total value of agriculture in the Waterloo Region of over $76,400,000 (1976), these infrastructure adjustments - amortised over 20 years - are trivial. The planning for Mennonite transportation required 10 days of professional effort. For tourism alone, these minor professional expenditures are clearly justified; the Mennonite Farmers Market has tens of thousands of customers, and they come by horse, by car, by truck and by bus.

Facility Development Mode

Facility development, such as highway, pipeline, waste disposal site, or nuclear plant are site specific developments which impact selectively on adjacent landowners, and as well may produce external impacts such as downstream erosion. The utilisation of EM comes in the form of environmental assessments, followed by environmental inspection as part of the environmental protection phase (environmental inspection falls under the construction phase in Figure 1).

The cost of doing an environmental assessment report is in the range of 10-15 per cent of the total planning and engineering design. As a percentage of the total construction costs, planning and engineering fees may be 1 per cent approximately. Thus EM is not expensive unless it delays approvals.

The benefits are of two kinds. One benefit is to stop the project because it is not safe or reasonable to build; projects which "die" in this manner are not visible to the public but it is fair to say that if the project is killed on the grounds of EM analysis then the ensuing environmental damage would have far outweighed any costs to do the studies or to undertake the mitigation required. The second benefit comes from savings generated internal to the design and development of the project. These savings can be found in the following areas: generation of better alternatives, generation of a biophysical data base which allows for more precise contract specifications and better competitive bidding, better analysis of damage claims to injured parties because of the baseline data available to measure the precise conditions existing before development began. Offset against the costs of doing an environmental assessment, benefits exceed costs about 10 to 1 (Dorney, 1986). It is for these reasons that we now see little hostility to the concept of doing environmental assessments for private development projects. Resistance resides in the government departments which wish to control their own mandates and not allow "new Ministries" to encroach on their territory. In view of the cost-effectiveness, this resistance within Ministries will recede over time under pressure from those who control the purse - the Ministries of Treasury and Finance. The only caveat in this discussion is the element of time; any unreasonable delays in approvals or hearings can quickly erode any benefits arising from the environmental assessment procedure. Analysis of environmental assessments can be facilitated by reference to a list of technical items to test the thoroughness of the work (Dorney and Hoffman, 1979).

SUMMARY AND CONCLUSIONS

In this brief paper some of the cost-effectiveness of EM has been sketched out. Although this profession is relatively new, it has come a long way in developing methodologies and procedures appropriate to the issue at hand, whether it is a policy issue or a development issue. To be effective it requires local expertise, and a local (regional or urban scale) data base. This means that for many Third World countries, local universities and regionally based government personnel form a vital link which cannot be substituted for a central state planning agency approach. If EM policy formulation is done at the central level, and urban and regional development and facility development handled at the local level, a higher degree of cost-effectiveness likely will be achieved. In any case, the value of EM can be measured in monetary terms - and it comes out rather well considering its "tender age".

As training and expertise improve, EM should become better established and more effectively utilised by business leaders and political leaders, and by lending agencies which want a relatively risk free return on investment.

REFERENCES

Dorney, R.S. (1973) "Role of ecologists as consultants in urban planning," *Human Ecology*, 1: 183-200.
Dorney, R.S. (1977a) "Biophysical and cultural-historic land classification and mapping for Canadian urban and urbanising land," in *Ecological (Biophysical) Land Classification in Urban Areas*, Ecological Land Classification, Series No. 3, Environment Canada, Ottawa, pp. 57-71.

Dorney, R.S. (1977b) "Planning for environmental quality in Canada: perspectives for the future," Major Theme Paper presented to the Canadian Institute of Planners, Annual Meeting, Toronto (copies available from the author).

Dorney, R.S. (1986) "The professional practice of environmental management," Waterloo: University of Waterloo, Faculty of Environmental Studies, unpublished manuscript.

Dorney, R.S., Evered, B. and Kitchen, C.M. (1986) "Tree conservation in the urbanising fringe of southern Ontario cities," *Urban Ecology*, 9: 289-308.

Dorney, R.S. and Hoffman, D.W. (1979) "Development of landscape planning concepts and management strategies for an urbanising agricultural region," *Landscape Planning*, 6: 151-77.

Dorney, R.S. and Wagner-McLellan, P. (1984) "The urban ecosystem: its spatial structure, its scale relationships, and its subsystem attributes," *Environments*, 16: 9-20.

Flannery, K.V. (ed.) (1982) *Maya Subsistence: Studies in Memory of Denis E. Puleston*, New York: Academic Press.

LeBlanc, G.V. (1983) "An evaluation of land use planning policies and administrative structures in Ontario," Waterloo: University of Waterloo, School of Urban and Regional Planning, unpublished M.A. thesis.

Loucks, D.E., Perkowski, J. and Bowie, D.B. (1982) "The impact of environmental assessment on energy project development," Petro Canada, Calgary, Alberta, and York University, Downsview, Ontario.

National Energy Board (Canada) (1984) *1983 Annual Report*, Ottawa.

URBANIZATION AND THE ENVIRONMENT: PROJECT ECOVILLE

Christian M. Dufournaud
Department of Geography
University of Waterloo
Waterloo, Ontario

Joseph B.R. Whitney
Department of Geography and
Institute for Environmental Studies
University of Toronto
Toronto, Ontario

The purpose of this paper is to review the findings of Project Ecoville, which is based in the Institute for Environmental Studies of the University of Toronto. The purpose of this project is to study the *environmental consequences of urbanisation*. Its focus has been cities in the Third World because of their rapid growth rates and overcrowding. This paper will review some of the more interesting findings which have come out of the research effort.

The thrust of the research has focused on three interrelated questions concerning urbanisation and its environmental consequences. First, is rapid urbanisation inevitable in the Third World? Second, what are the environmental consequences of rapid urbanisation? Third, why is it that cities are generating environmental deterioration which is more harmful (in some sense) than an equivalent population less concentrated in space? An important underlying theme in this research has been to try to develop better policies which can counteract the environmental degradation which urbanisation generates, without, in the process, hindering the economic and social development sought by the inhabitants of Third World nations. In addition to this, the members of Project Ecoville

have paid close attention to operationalising the research effort in
order to model comprehensively the complex interactions and
feedbacks characterising the urbanising process.

Ecoville research has been carried out worldwide by research
teams in the Third World. However, the Toronto group has been
closely associated with research in two countries: Senegal and the
Sudan, and work related to these two countries is now being
published. A simulation model of the flows and interactions between
subsystems in the case of Dakar, Senegal, and for the entire country,
in the case of the Sudan, have been developed. In addition a similar
model has been developed for the metropolitan area of the city of
Toronto. The simulation approach is the best way to integrate the
many variables which causally drive the urbanisation process. The
specific simulation approach adopted by Ecoville relies on the
Adaptive Environmental Assessment and Management approach
(AEAM) by Holling and his associate (1980). This approach involves
the participation of the relevant decision makers, disciplinary experts
and computer programmers who jointly formulate objectives,
indicators to measure progress towards these objectives and the
simulation model which interrelates in an operational manner the
variables. The completed simulation model is then run under
different policy scenarios so that the decision makers can determine
optimal policies. It is described as follows:

$$x(t+1) - x(t) = A(t)x(t) + B(t)u(t) \qquad (1)$$

$$A(t+1) = f(x(t+1),u(t)) \qquad (2)$$

$$B(t+1) = g(x(t+1),u(t)) \qquad (3)$$

u(t) interactively alterable.

In the above questions, x represents a vector of *state* variables
which describe the system at any given time period, u represents a
vector of *control* variables which the policy-maker can alter to achieve
predetermined goals and A and B represent the coefficients which
program the temporal transition. Thus, equation (1) says that the
change in the state variables in one time period is a function of the
current values of the state variables, the current values of the control
variables and the current values of the coefficients. Equations (2) and
(3) determine the feedback mechanisms in the model. These
equations ·say that the coefficients will change as a function of the
newly determined values of the state variables in the following year

and the control variables in the current year. Lastly, the values of u, at any given time period, are under the control of a planner.

CASE STUDIES

The Senegal Model

The primary objective of the Senegal Model was to replicate the population growth rate of the city of Dakar by modelling both the immigration and natural population increases (White and Dufournaud, 1984). The model defined the number of people moving into Dakar as a state variable and the interregional distribution of public expenditure as a control variable. The causal mechanism for migration was that people would move from regions exhibiting low per capita incomes to regions exhibiting the contrary condition. In addition to this, interregional multipliers were assumed to operate, such that all public funds spent outside of Dakar would generate an income effect within the region but also within Dakar. Outmigration from Dakar was set at zero but inmigration was allowed to vary in accordance with the above mentioned mechanism. One of the scenarios was to increase public expenditures outside of Dakar to the point where all urban inmigration ceased. This simulation indicated that the greatest proportion of multipliers generated growth in Dakar thus, biasing migration towards that centre regardless of the amount of investments made elsewhere in the other regions. It appears that no policy of investment redistribution could diminish the flow of migrants into Dakar. This finding is interesting because it is generally assumed that one way of controlling the migration component of urban growth is regional investment. Our initial findings cast doubt on this assumption.

The Sudan Model

The primary purpose of the Sudan Model (Murck et al., 1985) was to investigate the impact of changes in urban energy demand on fuel imports and on environmental deterioration. The underlying premise of the model is that as per capita incomes rise, there is a twofold change in consumption patterns: first, there is greater per capita consumption and secondly, there is substitution of consumption, the latter effect according to the well known Engel law. In this first modelling exercise we concentrated primarily on the energy factor.

The simulation model involved the use of an Input/Output table to trace the environmental consequences of final consumption. The principal policy alternative examined in this first attempt was the introduction of more efficient charcoal burning stoves into urban households. It is often assumed that more efficient stoves will result in slower rates of deforestation and hence will reduce the amount of environmental deterioration. Contrary to expectations, our initial results indicate that the amount of deforestation is far less than expected and the overall demand for energy, particularly fossil fuels, actually rises. This is because household savings resulting from more efficient stoves is spent on other items which impose increased burdens on the energy production sector including wood fuel. It follows from the above that any policy which, directly or indirectly, raises a person's income will cause greater environmental stress.

Although the above policy is socially beneficial since it gives households greater disposable income (unless charcoal is purchased), it is clearly not one that will produce the desired environmental benefits and further policy alternatives are now being modelled (Whitney et al., 1985).

The Toronto Model

The AEAM methodology was employed to construct a simulation model of the Toronto region with the expectation that, in modified forms, it could serve as a framework for similar models in Third World cities. The Toronto model (Whitney and Jones, 1983) is designed to investigate the interrelationships among inmigration, income distribution and unemployment and health status in the Toronto region under different investment policies. Our preliminary studies showed that health status (Baxter, 1984) is more directly related to socio-economic variables than to environmental factors. The model contains an Input/Output table which generates the effects of both public and private investments on income distribution, household formation and health status. The public investments include: local, provincial and federal policies, the latter specifically related to inmigration as exogenous variables.

Other Ecoville Projects

The Ecoville network includes members in Latin America and Asia. Among these, the Kuala Lumpur and Shanghai groups are in the process of building models specifically designed to investigate problems of air pollution and solid waste management. In addition to the modelling work discussed above, the Ecoville Project has undertaken, with the financial assistance of SSHRC and IDRC, a major project in Africa studying the delivery of urban services.

COUNTRIES PARTICIPATING IN THE ECOVILLE NETWORK

AFRICA: Ivory Coast, Kenya, Nigeria, Senegal, Sudan, Tanzania, Zaire.

ASIA: China, Hong Kong, Indonesia, Japan, Korea, Malaysia, Philippines, Singapore, Sri Lanka, Thailand.

LATIN AMERICA: Brazil, Chile, Columbia, Ecuador, Mexico, Venezuela.

EUROPE AND NORTH AMERICA: Canada, United Kingdom, United States.

OTHER: Australia.

REFERENCES

Baxter, D. (1984) *Health in the Urban Environment: Health Status Indicators and Their Use in Measuring Quality of Life*, Toronto: University of Toronto, Institute for Environmental Studies, Project Ecoville, Discussion Paper No. 10.

Holling, C. (1980) *Adaptive Environmental Assessment and Management*, New York: John Wiley and Sons.

Murck, B., Dufournaud, C. and Whitney, J. (1985) "Simulation of a policy aimed at the reduction of wood use in the Sudan," *Environment and Planning*, (in press).

White, R. and Dufournaud, C. (1984) *Modelling the Environmental Implications of Third World Urbanization: A Case Study of Dakar Senegal*, Toronto: University of Toronto, Institute for Environmental Studies, Project Ecoville, Discussion Paper No. 13.

Whitney, J. and Jones, M. (1983) *The Ecoville Toronto Simulation Model*, Toronto: University of Toronto, Institute for Environmental Studies, Project Ecoville, Discussion Paper No. 8.

Whitney, J, Dufournaud, C. and Murck, B. (1985) *An Examination of Alternate Energy Use Strategies in the Sudan*, Toronto: University of Toronto, Institute for Environmental Studies, unpublished paper to appear in the Project Ecoville Discussion Paper Series.

THE ENVIRONMENTAL IMPACT OF ENERGY USE ON FOREST RESOURCES: ST. LUCIA

Paul F. Wilkinson
Faculty of Environmental Studies
York University
Toronto, Ontario

INTRODUCTION

Over the past several years, worldwide concern about the availability and cost of energy has led to a growing interest in national patterns of energy consumption in the hope that wiser policies for energy use will emerge from a better understanding of existing patterns of energy consumption within and among nations. Most research to date has focused on the industrialised nations, partly because their policies have the greatest impact on world energy consumption (Fernandez, 1980). Patterns of energy consumption in less developed countries, however, are also of interest in terms of not only their relationship to world energy consumption, but also the role of energy within their economies and its impact on prospects for social and economic development. There is also a growing interest in the physical and ecological impacts of energy consumption patterns, particularly in terms of increasing desertification in many parts of Africa as a result of firewood gathering. Despite well-documented historical effects (e.g. Aruba), one topic that has received very little attention, however, is that of the impact of energy consumption patterns on very small, tropical island nations with limited resource base. There are approximately twenty such nations in the world belonging to the United Nations, with populations under one million and a per capita gross domestic product (GDP) of less than CDN$3,000. This paper will briefly explore this problem using St. Lucia and household energy consumption as a case study.

Such nations are faced with severe energy problems, compounded by four factors:

1. Serious balance of payments deficits and the inability to meet payment schedules for foreign loans, frequently related to a great degree to energy import bills which continue to escalate despite slow or negative economic growth;
2. Even when there is positive economic growth, it has been found that total energy consumption increases logarithmically with a nation's gross national product at lower gross domestic product levels (Brookes, 1972);
3. These very small nations have limited domestic stocks of traditional (i.e. nonrenewable, petroleum-based) energy resources; and
4. While there have been numerous attempts at providing alternative energy supplies from domestic renewable sources (e.g. firewood, solar, wind, geothermal), there is little evidence that such alternate energy sources are replacing imported fuels, as opposed to providing additional energy or to providing energy in areas or for uses not currently served by nonrenewable fuels (e.g. the use of solar driers in agriculture).

As a result of these factors, many countries have begun to examine their energy situations in order to develop a coherent energy policy which would help them to meet several possible goals: to stabilise or even to decrease their dependence on foreign energy payments; to decrease the use of energy or at least the rate of growth of use; to increase domestic production of energy from either traditional or nontraditional sources.

The development of such a national policy requires the input of a wide range of background data, e.g. domestic energy production and potential resources, energy imports, consumption patterns. In theory, it also requires analysis of the environmental impacts of energy consumption, but in practice these are frequently omitted. The reasons are complex. They include lack of trained personnel, cost, awareness, etc. It is suggested that a major influence is the traditional approach of international aid agencies (particularly the World Bank) which seem to be tied to helping such nations plan for petroleum-based energy, while ignoring the impacts on the environment and alternative energy sources.

THE SETTING

St. Lucia, a self-governing nation in the Windward Islands of the Lesser Antilles, is a small (616 km²) mountainous island of volcanic origin, with a maximum elevation of 1,000 m; there is little flat land. The climate is tropical marine, with vegetation ranging from Mediterranean to rain forest, depending on orientation, topography, and the steep precipitation gradient (1500-3500 mm). There are no known mineral resources, although there are active thermal springs of questionable geothermal potential.

With a population of approximately 118,000 almost equally divided between urban and rural areas, St. Lucia is extremely densely settled (292 persons per km² of arable land). It has a relatively diversified economy; agriculture (bananas), tourism, and regional manufacturing. The GDP per capita (CDN$842 in 1982) is one of the lowest in the Caribbean region; there is a serious balance of payments deficit (33 per cent of GDP in 1982). Petroleum products represent approximately 10 per cent of the value of imports.

THE ENERGY SITUATION

Unpublished 1977 World Bank estimates of secondary energy use in St. Lucia purport to show that 90 per cent of the nation's energy is obtained from petroleum either directly or indirectly in the form of electricity produced by diesel generators. These data estimate that only 5.6 per cent (0.622×10^{14} J of equivalent heat values) is obtained from charcoal; firewood was entirely omitted from the estimates. This picture is striking in light of global figures. Wood is the fourth largest source of energy in the world after petroleum, coal, and natural gas (Hyman, 1983); and 2,000 million people in the world depend on fuelwood as their major domestic energy source (FAO, 1982). Similarly, it has been estimated that fuelwood and charcoal supply up to 80 per cent of the domestic energy used in rural areas in the Caribbean (Hinrichsen, 1981).

It is suggested that the use of considerable quantities of these fuels does not show up in official statistics because the charcoal and firewood markets are informally organised and there is an unknown amount of tree felling for fuel purposes. The problem has increased in the last few years with the rising cost of electricity and Liquid Petroleum Gas (LPG), resulting in increased demand and higher costs for charcoal, particularly in urban markets. For example the price of charcoal rose by a factor of 5 in St. Lucia in 1981. As a result of higher charcoal costs, many poorer, nonurban people have been priced out of the charcoal market and are increasingly turning to firewood. Deforestation - caused by cutting for firewood and charcoal and by expansion of agricultural land - is a serious problem with approximately 8 per cent of the forest cover being removed per annum; the natural regeneration rate of the present forest cover is approximately 5 per cent. Concern over the environmental effects of deforestation is therefore closely related to the use of charcoal and wood for energy in St. Lucia, as it is in many Third World nations (Eckholm, 1975, 1976). This illustrates the way in which energy is intimately tied to a broader set of problems with major social, institutional, and environmental implications, for example, landholding patterns, soil conservation, erosion, increased stream sedimentation, etc.

These suppositions about energy use in St. Lucia were borne out by the results of a household energy survey undertaken by the Government of St. Lucia (Wilkinson, 1985); only some of the major conclusions will be related here. Charcoal was used by 88 per cent of all households, including 80 per cent of urban and 79 per cent of higher income households. Firewood was used by 43 per cent of all households, with significantly higher use by nonurban and low income households. In general, energy use has increased in the past few years, particularly in terms of electricity, LPG, and charcoal. The pattern is very different, however, for lower-income and nonurban households; having been priced out of the market for both commercial fuels and charcoal, they are depending more on firewood. In total, charcoal and firewood account for approximately 53 per cent of household energy use. It is estimated that charcoal accounts for 1.823×10^{14} of equivalent heat value, approximately three times the World Bank estimate. The discrepancy for firewood is even more startling, for the World Bank did not even include firewood in its figures; it is estimated that firewood accounts for 0.820×10^{14} In sum, charcoal and firewood would therefore represent 20-25 per cent of the nation's energy, not the 5.6 per cent noted above.

SEARCHING FOR A SOLUTION

There is some room for optimism in that the magnitude of this problem is being recognised by both the St. Lucian Government and the World Bank. With the support of the Canadian International Development Agency, the St. Lucia Forestry Division has just completed a forest management plan which proposes a policy for optimum land use and a management system, based on sustained yields, for both public and private forest lands. The plan recommends an afforestation program for commercial timber and a smaller program for establishing short-rotation fuelwood plantations (mainly *leucaena leucocephala*). The results of the household energy research noted above have been incorporated into the World Bank's recent study of energy in St. Lucia (UNDP/World Bank, 1984), although the report concentrates on petroleum-based energy and electricity production. The World Bank also supports the notion of upgrading and expanding the Forestry Division so that it could implement such programs and monitor more closely charcoal production.

The problem has at least now been recognised: a data base exists, policy has been suggested, and institutional changes recommended. Implementation, however, will be costly and is certainly beyond the financial and current personnel capability of St. Lucia; international aid will be required. It remains to be seen how agencies such as the World Bank will react when faced with requests to finance solutions such as these which are beyond their traditional market economy approach to energy issues.

REFERENCES

Brookes, L.G. (1972) "Further thoughts on energy and economic growth," *Industrial Marketing Management*, 1(2): 262-63.

Eckholm, E. (1975) *The Other Energy Crisis: Firewood*, Washington, D.C.: Worldwatch Institute.

Eckholm, E. (1976) *Losing Ground: Environmental Stress and World Food Prospects*, New York: Norton.

Fernández, J.C. (1980), "Household energy use in non-OPEC developing countries," *Rand Publication Series No. R-2515-DOE*, Santa Monica: Rand Corporation.

Food and Agriculture Organization of the United Nations (FAO) (1982) *FAO'S Medium-term Objectives and Programmes in Forestry: Summary*, Rome: FAO.

Hinrichsen, D. (1981) "Energy resources in the wider Caribbean," *Ambio*, 10: 332-34.

Hyman, E.L. (1983) "How to conduct a rural energy survey in a developing country," *Renewable Sources of Energy*, 1(2): 137-49.

United Nations Development Program/World Bank, (1984) "St. Lucia: issues and options in the energy sector," *Report No. 5111-SLU of the Joint UNDP/World Bank Energy Sector Assessment Program*.

Wilkinson, P.F. (1985) "Energy resources in a Third World microstate: St. Lucia household energy survey," *Resources and Energy*, 6: 305-28.

CHAPTER 11

TRAINING

ARCHAEOLOGY, CULTURAL RESOURCE MANAGEMENT AND THIRD WORLD DEVELOPMENT: BELIZE, CENTRAL AMERICA

Paul F. Healy
Department of Anthropology
Trent University
Peterborough, Ontario

ARCHAEOLOGY AND DEVELOPMENT

The development of cultural resources, such as archaeological sites (prehistoric and historic), is a major concern of many nations, but particularly Third World countries. It is an area of interest by the latter group because such finite, nonrenewable resources often provide the only objective measure of their local history, and a significant, tangible focus for what is often new national pride. It is also a concern for poorer and smaller nations because they generally lack the funds or expertise necessary for conducting large scale archaeological investigations to begin with, for the caring and housing of artifactual remains recovered, or the protecting of archaeological sites discovered by such investigations. Consequently, many developing nations must rely almost totally upon foreign (usually North American or European) professionals to conduct this research, and to help develop their archaeological resources.

This pattern of foreign reliance for the development of the "patrimony" has produced some serious and rather adverse effects. Archaeological remains which are excavated by foreign projects, for example, are often exported for study and display, there generally being inadequate facilities in the Third World country of origin. New sites which are opened and cleared for investigations become obvious targets for looting, following research, to obtain valuable artifacts for foreign art markets. Furthermore, the lack of adequately trained local personnel to deal with the cultural resources has meant that an area of great potential for development (as in tourism) has often been lost.

Until recently this has been the case for the small, newly independent nation of Belize.

ARCHAEOLOGY AND BELIZE

Belize, formerly British Honduras, is a small (8,600 m²) underdeveloped British Commonwealth country in Central America. There are approximately 159,000 inhabitants (1980 census) composed of White, Creole, Carib, Mestizo, and Maya Indian groups. It is an exceedingly heterogeneous nation with many smaller ethnic groups (Chinese, Lebanese, East Indians, and Africans) also present. Belize became independent of Great Britain in September 1981. It lies in an area of several different spheres of political influence. It is clearly part, geographically, of Central America. However, its British, English-speaking heritage ties it closely with many Caribbean nations, such as Jamaica, and certainly to the British Commonwealth at large.

Foreign archaeological interest in Belize dates to the nineteenth century. From earliest European settlement, the presence of massive, sprawling Maya ruins were known. Early investigations, particularly by British Colonial Officials, brought such sites to the attention of the world. Large quantities of ancient Maya art, in the form of monumental stone carvings (stelae), jade ornaments, and beautifully painted Classic Maya ceramics, were removed from Belize and exported abroad. Most of these archaeological treasures are still housed outside Belize today.

Since the early 1960s there has been a particularly marked upsurge in foreign archaeological activity in Belize. This is due to at least three factors: (a) Belize's relative political stability compared to neighbouring regions of Central America; (b) the fact that the structure and attitudes characteristic of the Belize government have produced a high level of cooperation between foreign archaeologists and local authorities; and (c) the belated realisation that Belize was not a peripheral zone of the Classic Maya civilization, but an active, heavily populated region of the Lowland Maya heartland.

With the independence of Belize now a reality, there is a genuine interest by Belizeans in understanding their early history, in preserving their national heritage, and in being better able to care for and develop the cultural resources of their homeland. These are notable and praiseworthy goals, and objectives which stand to benefit not only Belize but the rest of the world as well. There is no question that the archaeological resources of this small, fledgling country are some of the most spectacular and significant anywhere in the western hemisphere, and deserving of special attention.

TRENT-ROM-CIDA TRAINING PROGRAM

In 1978, Trent University, in collaboration with the Royal Ontario Museum (ROM) and the Belize Department of Archaeology, reached agreement on the creation of a long term Canadian training program in Archaeology and Cultural Resource Management (CRM) tailored to fit the needs, and goals, of the Belize government. Funding for the six year program was granted by the Canadian International Development Agency (CIDA) in 1979, at a total cost of $350,000, of which CIDA donated one half. The program, now in its penultimate year, has been extremely successful and is an outstanding example of cooperation between Canada and a small, emerging Third World nation (Healy, 1981).

Indeed, Canada has a lengthy history of intimate involvement with the discovery and development of archaeological resources in Belize through major research activities of the Royal Ontario Museum, and more recently, Trent University. The Training Program has served to reinforce the Belize-Canada relationship of cooperation.

THE PROGRAM OBJECTIVES

The stated objectives of the Trent-ROM-CIDA training program were:

1. To provide technical and academic training in archaeology and culture resource management for Belizeans who have demonstrated their abilities in a range of areas and who are (or will become) part of the staff of the Belize Department of Archaeology;
2. To fill staffing needs at all levels; and
3. To provide the knowledge and skills necessary to preserve the nation's archaeological resources and develop Belize's archaeological potential.

The objectives of the program were met through a cluster of autonomous, but obviously interrelated, projects which were directed toward satisfying the goals noted. These separate projects can be classified as follows:

1. university training
2. field training
3. technical training
4. conservator training, and

5. caretaker/guide training.

Since 1979, this Canadian-sponsored program has provided financial assistance and trained two Belizeans to the M.A. degree, and three others to the B.A. degree level. When the programs began, there were no Belizeans employed in their Department of Archaeology with *any* formal training in archaeology, and a serious deficiency of trained supervisory personnel to administer the Department has been corrected. In the coming year it is expected that at least one additional Belizean will receive graduate level training in conservation and museology to oversee this work in a new national museum which is currently in the planning stage, while another student will complete an honours B.A. degree.

Aside from academic instruction in archaeology, four supervisory staff of the Belize Department of Archaeology have received formal training in field methods and techniques through a funded on-site apprenticeship project. The Belizean students participated on a variety of professionally staffed archaeological field projects to gain practical experience, under supervision, and to complement their university classroom instruction.

One of the primary objectives of the Belize Department of Archaeology is the preservation of ancient monuments, including the consolidation and restoration of prehistoric architecture. This requires quite specialised training in masonry. Given the large number of standing Maya ruins, some of great size, in Belize technical training was provided to approximately twelve Belizean workers, on the Department of Archaeology labourers crew, to enable them to consolidate and restore archaeological ruins in an accurate, and touristically appealing, fashion. Part of the practical training has included several one month apprenticeships on archaeological restoration projects in Mexico, where some of the best architectural rehabilitation of prehistoric sites has been done.

As the Belize Department of Archaeology is faced almost daily with problems of artifact conservation, there was an obvious and urgent need for staff instruction in conservation, and the establishment (if only minimally) of a conservation facility within the offices of the Department. The training program provided staff instruction by a professional Canadian conservator through a four month long course held in Belize. As noted above, a second stage of this aspect of the program will involve graduate training in Canada of a Belizean in conservation/museology.

Lastly the training program has provided formal instruction in Belize to archaeological site caretakers and guides. Prior to the Trent-

ROM-CIDA program, these local site guides had received no special training or education on the archaeology of Belize since the Department of Archaeology was not budgeted funds for such work. Yet, each of the ten caretakers/guides provided a critical government presence at the sites, and were the principal contact people for foreign tourists. Visitors today will be provided with a clearer, more accurate picture of Belize prehistory. Not only will this improve the perception tourists gain of Belize, but will have an immediate positive impact on local visitors to these same sites.

CONCLUSIONS

An increasing interest has arisen in providing aid for the development of programs to improve the archaeological training of local professionals (Miller, 1980). As the world economy has slowed down in the last decade, poor Third World nations have been faced with severe problems of dealing with, and managing, what are often spectacular cultural resources (Keatinge, 1980; Miller, 1980; Tamplin, 1981; White, 1982). Professional archaeologists from developed nations have become increasingly concerned about how to help resolve these problems, and have noted the ethical responsibilities to help protect, restore, and preserve the sites with which they are associated (Healy, 1984). The Trent-ROM-CIDA Training Program in Archaeology and Culture Resource Management for Belize is one example of Canadian efforts to improve the knowledge, education levels, and technical skills of staff in one small, Third World country, in order that they might better preserve their nation's rich archaeological resources more effectively and successfully. The impact of the Canadian program in Belize will be felt for years to come, and unquestionably will aid in the development of Belize's potential for international tourism. The economic significance of the latter should not be underestimated. Neighbouring Mexico, for example, has developed and managed its cultural resources so effectively that it is a major factor in their tourism. In fact, the tremendous income of foreign exchange through visitors has made tourism the largest single industry in Mexico, surpassing even its petroleum exports. The potential for Belize is equally promising if its cultural resources can be effectively managed, protected, and promoted.

REFERENCES

Healy, P.F. (1981) *Interim Report to the Canadian International Development Agency on the Trent University-Royal Ontario Museum-CIDA Training Program Archaeology and Culture Resource Management in Belize, 1978-1981*, Peterborough, Ontario: Trent University, Department of Anthropology, manuscript on file.

Healy, P.F. (1984) "Archaeology abroad: ethical considerations of fieldwork in foreign countries," in Green, E.L. (ed.), *Ethics and Values in Archaeology*, The Free Press (MacMillan), New York, pp. 123-32.

Keatinge, R.W. (1980) "Archaeology and development: the Templadera sites of the Peruvian north coast," *Journal of Field Archaeology*, 7: 467-75.

Miller, D. (1980) "Archaeology and development," *Current Anthropology*, 21: 709-26.

Tamplin, M.J. (1981) *Archaeology and Culture Resource Management*, paper presented at 10th Annual Meeting of the Canadian Archaeological Association, Calgary, Alberta.

White, P.T. (1982) "The Temples of Angkor: ancient glory in stone," *National Geographic*, 161: 552-89.

CHAPTER 12

INSTITUTIONAL ASPECTS

ROLE OF RESEARCH IN THIRD WORLD COUNTRIES

S. Imtiaz Ahmad
School of Computer Science
University of Windsor
Windsor, Ontario

INTRODUCTION

Research activity normally produces results which are cumulative in nature. The success in this activity depends on the ability of scientists to select problems which can be solved with conceptual and instrumental techniques close to those already in existence. Such success represents a step in the evolutionary process.

On the other hand, a sense of malfunction in time honoured theory and practice may cause a revolutionary change in research activity (Kuhn, 1970). In either case, the research institutions have a role to play in orchestrating research activity from planning to design, implementation and evaluation. These are complex tasks, particularly when one realises the difficulties in: (a) forecasting the direction of scientific development, and (b) controlling the mechanism intrinsic to scientific advances.

The planning process involves determining the needs which exist, gathering of information on available and expected resources and capabilities, and generating a set of alternatives for evaluation and commitment. In order to determine the needs, it is necessary that the existing problems be adequately articulated creating a climate conducive to change. The change alternatives are based on data about the past and the current trends including such things as the rate of adoption and innovation, capabilities to be developed, and also those capabilities which are required but not considered suitable for internal development.

The design process requires examining one or more alternatives in detail, and determining how the needs can be satisfied.

Furthermore, allocation of resources, organisation of tasks, expected results and ways of measuring performance must be considered.

Implementation of research activities makes the resources available to research institutions such as universities and research centres and creates conditions for diffusion of innovation and research productivity. In addition, it provides support for solving instrumental, conceptual and mathematical problems related to existing knowledge and techniques. Other considerations must also be taken into account including such things as peer evaluation and acceptance of solutions, sharing of these solutions by a well defined community of scientists, recognition of the existence of a uniquely competent professional group, and an acceptance of its role as the exclusive arbiter of professional achievement. Standard published accounts of solutions may not be adequate, necessitating the need for other forms of communications among the researchers.

Finally, the evaluation process, necessary to refine each activity described above, must be further applied to maintain a desired focus on research, and redirected to new areas, as the needs emerge.

The activities described above and their relationships are displayed in Figure 1.

PLANNING

Research institutions at the national level play a key role in planning for development (Chen, 1984). Planning requires knowledge about the following:

1. What are current activities?
2. What are the finished products of scientific achievement and the enterprises which produced them?
3. What are the needs of these enterprises, and what is their view of what is achievable?
4. What resources, including infrastructures, are required? What technology is required to support scientific research, and is that technology obtained internally, or obtained externally?
5. What are the differences or discrepancies between the anticipated and the actual performance of the ongoing planning activity and are these differences explainable by the models used in the planning process?

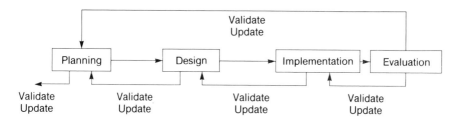

Figure 1: Roles of Research Institutions, Required Activities and Relationships

Not only must this knowledge be collected and represented, it must be appropriately structured to allow effective use and updating in response to changes. For example, capabilities may undergo enhancement or depletion, infrastructures or external technology may not materialise as expected, etc.

The planning activity must also take into account the interdisciplinary nature of the development process, i.e. development in one field is in some way related to developments in other fields.

Using one or more forecasting models suited to the environment (Martino, 1985) scenarios are generated. These scenarios may consist of short term projects or prototypes and long term research plans. Prototypes are necessary for articulation of the problems and needs, and preparing the groundwork for long term research activity. These prototypes provide ad-hoc solutions, ultimately leading to more realistic designs.

DESIGN

The research institution consisting of a national authority, universities and research centres is responsible for bringing in organisational changes necessary for research and development. The national authority, in particular, serves as a facilitator of research. It may create an advisory panel consisting of national, expatriate and foreign experts, knowledgeable about the research fields selected in the planning process. Moreover, it shows leadership in the transmission of relevant knowledge, complementing the role of universities, but taking it one step further by providing consultation in application of newly created relevant knowledge. It may arrange national forums and adopt other means of dissemination of this knowledge to users in mid-career, engaged in research and development, who may not have the necessary skills to implement and utilise innovations successfully. The national research institution may first take initiatives to bring a behavioural change toward these innovations by dissemination of information. Further articulation of users' needs occurs through this process, and through some participation in prototypes of anticipated research and development projects and environments, leading also to the identification of needs which may not have been considered earlier.

In this design process, alternatives generated by the planning process are elaborated, altered and fully specified in an iterative manner until acceptable solutions are developed, thus not only satisfying the planning and forecasting model but also relating to the environment in sufficient detail in order to allow a realistic implementation.

IMPLEMENTATION

The design process identifies what is reasonable within the country and what is required to conduct this research. It identifies domestic and imported technology support and other resources needed to conduct this research. The implementation process translates this design into physical realisation by simultaneously putting in place the facilities for domestic technology, and importing the technology which blends well with domestic capabilities and creates manpower for research and development. Implementation also puts in place mechanisms which allow diffusion of innovation, i.e. results of research and development get into widespread use. It creates a scientific community which encourages innovation and gives credibility to those who produce work of quality. It ensures that researchers work on problems which they have selected, eliminating barriers which waste researchers' time on nonproductive activities. It takes steps to develop an environment which meets researchers' requirements in a timely manner and on a sustained basis.

A national research institution can set up appropriate cells to facilitate and coordinate the implementation process in order to maintain the desired quality and maximise the utilisation of resources. The success of implementation should be evident from the measurable improvements in performance of the scientific enterprise.

EVALUATION

Standards for evaluating the performance are established prior to implementation. Discrepancies in the measured versus expected performance can result from planning, design, implementation or from the models which are used to measure performance. If problems are stemming from the implementation, they can be corrected on an ongoing basis until the desired performance level is achieved. In many cases, however, the problems with the performance may be due to errors in planning or design, and if so, will require substantially more effort to put the research enterprise on track.

The planning process starts with an initial data base being continually updated by the design, implementation and performance evaluation activities. This data base is a valuable information resource containing knowledge about the relevant objects and processes in the real world. Proper engineering of this knowledge determines how well the research institutions are able to fulfill their role. This data base should also be guarded against possible abuse by others.

The research projects are also evaluated at periodic intervals coinciding with expected completion dates, or milestones, marking major achievements. Without proper evaluation of the existing programs, new programs cannot be properly designed or implemented.

REFERENCES

Chen, K. (1984) "An analysis of research institutional roles in developing countries," *IEEE Trans. Systems, Man and Cybernetics*, SMC-14(3): 470-73.

Kuhn, T.S. (1970) *The Structure of Scientific Revolutions*, 2e, Chicago: The University of Chicago Press.

Martino, J.P. (1985) "Looking ahead with confidence," *IEEE Spectrum*, 22(3): 76-81.

RESOURCES AND THE ENVIRONMENT: THE NORTHERN ONTARIO EXPERIENCE AND ITS APPLICABILITY TO THE THIRD WORLD

Geoffrey R. Weller
Department of Political Studies
Lakehead University
Thunder Bay, Ontario

NORTHERN ONTARIO AS THIRD WORLD

Some almost direct parallels exist between the northern Ontario experience in terms of the relationship between resources and the environment and the experience of the Third World. This is largely because northern Ontario, like so many regions of the Third World, is an exploited resource hinterland (Miller, 1980; Scott, 1975; Wallace, 1982; Weller, 1977). In fact, a cogent argument can be made that the remote north of the province, along with similar regions in many other provinces, constitutes Canada's own internal Third World colony (Weller, 1984). Most Canadians would not accept, or wish to accept this, so a case has to be made briefly before turning to arguments concerning the relationship between resources and the environment.

Northern Ontario covers roughly 90 per cent of the land area of Ontario but has a population of only 800,000 or approximately 8 per cent of the provincial total. The population is divided between native peoples and whites. Many ethnic divisions exist among the white population. The native population is divided between status Indians, nonstatus Indians and Metis. Much of the area has a shield geology and a harsh climate both of which severely limit agriculture. The major industries of the region are forestry (mainly in northwestern Ontario), mining (mainly in northeastern Ontario), power generation, transportation and tourism. This combination clearly reflects the region's hinterland status as does the lack of cohesiveness among the population and in the economy. This hinterland status also reveals itself in many of the other ways one would expect if the centre-periphery model were applied internally or within a single political jurisdiction rather than between them as has normally been the case.[1] In this particular instance, "the centre" is construed as southern Ontario or the Golden Horseshoe area and "the periphery" is construed as all of northern Ontario.

As predicted by centre-periphery analysis there is a clear difference in economic and social well being between northern and southern Ontario. Even within the north there are two aspects and grossly unequal groupings. Those associated with the natural resource economy, largely the white population of the large cities and towns, are less well off than the southern population in general, and they tend to be more "blue collar". Those associated with the traditional hunting, fishing and trapping economy, largely the native population of the more remote small communities are very much less well off and there is a great deal of poverty, even extreme poverty, in many areas. The disparity between the north and the south, and within the north, is also clearly seen in health and education statistics (Thunder Bay District Health Council, 1978). The northern native population, in fact, has the disease pattern of the Third World Society caused not so much by a lack of health services but by the great poverty they experience (Weller, 1981).

The Centre-Periphery theory argues that a vertical set of relations develop between the Centre and the Periphery at the expense of interaction between or within peripheries and that this vertical set of relations embodies unequal trade benefits. This certainly seems to be the case in northern Ontario which is treated by the provincial centre as a "protected" region delivering products needed by the centre. This commodity specialisation leads to both a lack of interaction between northern Ontario and similar regions in other provinces and between the resource and traditional sectors of the northern Ontario economy. This is seen in the structure of the transportation network which is clearly designed to expedite the movement of raw materials to the centre rather than connections between the provincial norths or the various parts of northern Ontario. The unequal nature of trade benefits results from manufactured goods being exchanged for raw materials to the benefit of the centre, not only directly, but in terms of the much greater degree of processing which takes place there with all its associated benefits. Since the objective of the Centre is to

----

[1] An interesting application of the internal colony approach was made in a similar nearby region in Bellfy (1977).

extract as many of the resources of northern Ontario as possible at least possible cost it is not surprising that little thought was given until recently to either the creation of a reasonably self-reliant regional economy and society or the environmental consequences of low cost resource extraction (Hutchinson and Wallace, 1977; Ontario Public Interest Research Group, 1976; Troyeer, 1977).

The single largest threat to the environment of northern Ontario comes from the forest industry. Some argue that the forests are being utilised as if they were a nonrenewable resource because they are being cut at a rate which makes full regeneration impossible (Lie, 1978). If this is indeed the case then at some point in the future the economy of much of the region will collapse as it did in an earlier period in the Upper Peninsula of Michigan. At another level the forest industry also damages the northern environment and society by seriously polluting some of the air and water of the region. The second largest set of environmental problems in northern Ontario have been caused by the mining industry which has created both air and water pollution in significant quantities (Swift, 1978). Other environmental problems are caused by the transportation industry including grain dust emissions and the movement of hazardous materials. Still other environmental problems are caused by or feared from the power generation industry. More recently there have also been fears about grandiose diversion plans for much of the water in the region to be redirected to the drier parts of the United States. It is clear that the resources of northern Ontario have been exploited, or are planned to be, for the use of others. That little thought is given to the environmental consequences can be seen in the various issues, such as the mercury contamination of the English-Wabigoon River System, which have achieved national and international notoriety (Weller, 1980).

ONTARIO GOVERNMENT ACTION TO REDUCE CONFLICT OVER ENVIRONMENT

Conflict over environmental matters in northern Ontario in the late 1960s and 1970s led to something of a polarisation of forces for and against further development of resources based industries. Two sets of interests supported further development. Firstly, there were those that supported more of the same kind of development that existed already. Secondly, there were those who wished to see the kind of development that would change the hinterland status of the region. The groups which opposed further resource development in northern Ontario ranged from those who were not opposed to development per se but did not see the possibility of adequate environmental safeguards being adopted under the present economic structure of existing regulations to those groups that would really rather the north be an essentially wilderness area. The groups opposing development had nothing like the same resources as were possessed by those supporting development. They were organisationally more fragmented, financially less well off and without the same tradition of easy access to government.

The provincial and federal governments acted in the late 1970s and 1980s to reduce the conflict in northern Ontario over environmental matters. They attempted to promote diffuse political support by incorporating as many of the policy actors as possible into a search for policies that would involve compromises. They did this in many ways including the creation of new bureaucratic agencies (such as the Ministry of Northern Affairs), the encouragement of public participation in environmental policy making through many elaborate devices such as Royal Commissions (for example, the infamous Royal Commission on the Northern Environment), and a judicious mix of regulatory and distributive environmental policies in combination with a strongly stated commitment to "responsible" development. The result of these actions, along with the changing social and political climate, was that public discontent was largely defused and the worst abuses were stopped and some corrected. However, the fundamental exploitative relationship has not changed and the northern environment remains seriously threatened (Nord and Weller, 1983).

IMPLICATIONS FOR THE THIRD WORLD

The clear implication for Third World nations of the northern Ontario experience is to resist the entrenchment of the Centre-Periphery relationship and all that goes with it including vertical integration, commodity specialisation, low cost extraction to serve the interests of the Centre and not the Periphery, as well as dependence on high cost imported manufactured goods. The best way to do this is to exploit to the fullest extent the advantage that Third World nations have that northern Ontario does not, namely a political boundary. A political boundary and independent status means there is at least the possibility of resisting becoming the "protected" resource of a metropolitan centre as has become the case with northern Ontario. Linkages could be made with multiple metropolitan centres and with other less developed areas to resist the encroachments of metropolitan centres. Unless this is done the Centre will always try to extract resources at the lowest possible cost and this inevitably means that environmental concerns will not be paramount and may well be one of the last factors considered.

REFERENCES

Bellfy, P.G. (1977) "Michigan's upper peninsula: an internal colony," paper presented to the Michigan Sociological Association's Annual Meeting, Detroit, (April).

Hutchinson, G. and Wallace, D. (1977) *Grassy Narrows*, Toronto: Van Nostrand Reinhold.

Lie, K. (1978) "The plight of Ontario's northern forests," *Alternatives*, 7 (Autumn): pp. 17-25.

Miller, T. (1980) "Cabin fever: the province of Ontario and its norths," in MacDonald, D.C. (ed.), *Government and Politics of Ontario*, (2nd. ed.), Toronto: Van Nostrand Reinhold, pp. 227-44.

Nord, D.C. and Weller, G.R. (1983) "Environmental policy and political support," in Kornberg, A. and Clark, H.D. (eds.), *Political Support in Canada: The Crisis Years*, Durham, North Carolina: Duke University Press, pp. 252-69.

Ontario Public Interest Research Group (1976) *Quicksilver and Slow Death*, Toronto: OPIRG.

Scott, D. (1975) "Northern alienation," in MacDonald, D.C. (ed.), *Government and Politics of Ontario*, Toronto: MacMillan, pp. 235-48.

Swift, J. (1978) *The Big Nickel: Inco at Home and Abroad*, Kitchener: Between the Lines.

Thunder Bay District Health Council (1978) *Panorama of Mortality*, Thunder Bay: Thunder Bay District Health Council.

Troyeer, W. (1977) *No Safe Place*, Toronto: Clarke Irwin.

Wallace, I. (1982) "The Canadian Shield: the development of a research frontier," in McCann, L.D. (ed.), *Heartland and Hinterland: A Geography of Canada*, Scarborough, Ontario: Prentice Hall, pp. 372-409.

Weller, G.R. (1977) "Hinterland politics: the case of northwestern Ontario," *Canadian Journal of Political Science*, X(4) (December): 727-54.

Weller, G.R. (1980) "Resources development in northern Ontario: a case study in hinterland policies," in Dwivedi, O.P. (ed.), *Resources and the Environment: Policy Perspectives in Canada*, Toronto: McClelland and Stewart, pp. 243-69.

Weller, G.R. (1981) "The delivery of health care services in the Canadian North," *Journal of Canadian Studies*, 16(2): 69-80.

Weller, G.R. (1984) "Regional development in Canada: the case of the provincial north," paper delivered at the CPSA/AAPS conference on Regional Development in Canada and Africa, Harare, Zimbabwe (February).

RESOURCES AND ENVIRONMENT WORKSHOP PARTICIPANTS

S. Imtiaz Ahmad
School of Computer Science
University of Windsor
Windsor, Ontario, N9B 3P4

Jan Barica
National Water Research
 Institute
Canada Centre for Inland
 Waters
Burlington, Ontario, L7R 4A6

Rorke B. Bryan
University of Toronto
Scarborough Campus
1265 Military Trail
West Hill, Ontario, M1C 1A4

Bill Bruce
Canada Centre for Remote
 Sensing
2464 Sheffield Road
Ottawa, Ontario, K1A 0Y7

Robert G. Cecil
Department of Geography
University of Western Ontario
London, Ontario, N6A 5B8

Ward Chesworth
Department of Land Resource
 Science
University of Guelph
Guelph, Ontario, N1G 2W1

Ian K. Crain
Lands Directorate
Environment Canada
Place Vincent Massey, 21st Floor
Ottawa, Ontario, K1A 0E7

Robert S. Dorney
School of Urban and Regional
 Planning
University of Waterloo
Waterloo, Ontario, N2L 3G1

M.A. Faris
Research Scientist
Agriculture Canada
Ottawa Research Station
F.B. #12, CEF
Ottawa, Ontario, K1A 0G6

Christian M. Dufournaud
Department of Geography
University of Waterloo
Waterloo, Ontario, N2L 3G1

George R. Francis
Department of Environment
 and Resource Studies
University of Waterloo
Waterloo, Ontario, N2L 3G1

Christine Furedy
Division of Social Science
York University
4700 Keele Street
Downsview, Ontario, M3J 1P3

Murray Haight
School of Urban and Regional
 Planning
University of Waterloo
Waterloo, Ontario, N2L 3G1

Geoffrey Hainesworth
Institute for Research and
 Environmental Studies
Dalhousie University
Halifax, Nova Scotia, B3H 4H8

Paul F. Healy
Department of Anthropology
Trent University
Peterborough, Ontario, K9J 7B8

Jean-Claude Henein
Canada Centre for Remote
  Sensing
2464 Sheffield Road
Ottawa, Ontario, K1A 0Y7

Philip J. Howarth
Department of Geography
Faculty of Environmental Studies
University of Waterloo
Waterloo, Ontario, N2L 3G1

Nalni D. Jayal
Institute for Ecology Research
  and Environment Management
C11/13, Bapa Nagar, Dr.
Zakir Hussain Road
New Delhi - 110 003, India

Jofephath Kamasho
Uyole, College of Agriculture
Mbeya, Tanzania

K. Drew Knight
Faculty of Environmental Studies
University of Waterloo
Waterloo, Ontario, N2L 3G1

Ralph Kretz
Department of Geology
University of Ottawa
Ottawa, Ontario, K15 5B6

V. Chris Lakhan
Department of Geography
University of Windsor
Windsor, Ontario, N9B 3P4

Alexander G. McLellan
Department of Geography
University of Waterloo
Waterloo, Ontario, N2L 3G1

Evelyne S. Meltzer
International Centre for
  Ocean Development
11-1544 Summer Street
Halifax Nova Scotia,
B3H 3A4

S. Mengestou
Department of Biology
University of Waterloo
161 University Ave. W.
Apt. 110
Waterloo, Ontario, N2L 3E5

J. Gordon Nelson
Faculty of Environmental
  Studies
University of Waterloo
Waterloo, Ontario, N2L 3G1

Simsek Pala
Ontario Centre for Remote
  Sensing
Ontario Ministry of Natural
  Resources
880 Bay Street, 3rd Floor
Toronto, Ontario, M5S 1Z8

George Priddle
Department of Environment
  and Resource Studies
University of Waterloo
Waterloo, Ontario, N2L 3G1

Calvin Pride
International Development
  Research Centre
Box 8500
Ottawa, Ontario, K1G 3H9

Richard Protz
Department of Land Resource
  Science
University of Guelph
Guelph, Ontario, N1G 2W1

Henry A. Regier
Institute for Environmental
  Studies
University of Toronto
Toronto, Ontario, M5S 1A3

Johnson M.R. Semoka
Department of Soil Science
Sokoine University of
  Agriculture
Morogoro, Tanzania

Ihor Stebelsky
Department of Geography
University of Windsor
Windsor, Ontario, N9B 3PA

Jean Thie
Lands Directorate
Environment Canada
Ottawa, Ontario, K1A 0E7

J. Kenneth Torrance
Department of Geography
Carleton University
Ottawa, Ontario, K1V 9W6

Mousseau Tremblay
Cooperative Programs Division
International Development
  Research Centre
Box 8500
Ottawa, Ontario, K1G 3H9

Peter van Straaten
Department of Land Resource
  Science
University of Guelph
Guelph, Ontario, N1G 2W1

Raúl Vicencio
Cooperative Programs Division
International Development
  Research Centre
Box 8500
Ottawa, Ontario, K1G 3H9

Jinfei Wang
Faculty of Environmental Studies
University of Waterloo
Waterloo, Ontario, N2L 3G1

Peter R. Waylen
Department of Geography
University of Saskatchewan
Saskatoon, Saskatchewan
S7N 0W0

Geoffrey R. Weller
Department of Political Studies
Lakehead University
Thunder Bay, Ontario
P7B 5E1

Joseph B.R. Whitney
Department of Geography
University of Toronto
Toronto, Ontario, M5S 1A3

Paul F. Wilkinson
Faculty of Environmental
  Studies
York University
4700 Keele Street
Downsview, Ontario, M4N 1P3

Ming-ko Woo
Department of Geography
McMaster University
1200 Main Street West
Hamilton, Ontario, L8S 4K1

University of Waterloo
Department of Geography Publication Series

Available from Publications, Department of Geography, University of Waterloo, Waterloo, Ontario, N2L 3Gl

26 WALKER, David F., 1987, *Manufacturing in Kitchener-Waterloo: A Long-Term Perspective*, ISBN 0-921083-22-X, 220 pp.
25 GUELKE, Leonard, 1986, *Waterloo Lectures in Geography, Vol. 2, Geography and Humanistic Knowledge*, ISBN 0-921083-21-1, 101 pp.
24 BASTEDO, Jamie, D. 1986, *An ABC Resource Survey Method for Environmentally Significant Areas with Special Reference to Biotic Surveys in Canada's North*, ISBN 0-921083-20-3, 135 pp.
23 BRYANT, Christopher, R., 1984, *Waterloo Lectures in Geography, Vol. 1, Regional Economic Development*, ISBN 0-921083-19-X, 115 pp.
22 KNAPPER, Christopher, GERTLER, Leonard, and WALL, Geoffrey, 1983, *Energy, Recreation and the Urban Field*, ISBN 0-921083-18-1, 89 pp.
21 DUDYCHA, Douglas J., SMITH, Stephen L.J., STEWART, Terry O., and McPHERSON, Barry D., 1983, *The Canadian Atlas of Recreation and Exercise*, ISBN 0-921083-17-3, 61 pp.
20 MITCHELL, Bruce, and GARDNER, James S., 1983, *River Basin Management: Canadian Experiences*, ISBN 0-921083-16-5, 443 pp.
19 GARDNER, James S., SMITH, Daniel J., and DESLOGES, Joseph R., 1983, *The Dynamic Geomorphology of the Mt. Rae Area: A High Mountain Region in Southwestern Alberta*, ISBN 0-921083-15-7, 237 pp.
18 BRYANT, Christopher R., 1982, *The Rural Real Estate Market: Geographical Patterns of Structure and Change in an Urban Fringe Environment*, ISBN 0-921083-14-9, 153 pp.
17 WALL, Geoffrey, and KNAPPER, Christopher, 1981, *Tutankhamun in Toronto*, ISBN 0-921083-13-0, 113 pp.
16 WALKER, David F., editor, 1980, *The Human Dimension in Industrial Development*, ISBN 0-921083-12-2, 124 pp.
15 PRESTON, Richard E., and RUSSWURM, Lorne H., editors, 1980, *Essays on Canadian Urban Process and Form II*, 505 pp. (Available only in microfiche).

14 WALL, Geoffrey, editor, 1979, *Recreational Land Use in Southern Ontario*, ISBN 0-921083-11-4, 374 pp.

13 MITCHELL, Bruce, GARDNER, James S., COOK, Robert, and VEALE, Barbara, 1978, *Physical Adjustments and Institutional Arrangements for the Urban Flood Hazard: Grand River Watershed*, ISBN 0-921083-10-6, 142 pp.

12 NELSON, J. Gordon., NEEDHAM, Roger D., and MANN, Donald, editors, 1978, *International Experience with National Parks and Related Reserves*, ISBN 0-921083-09-2, 624 pp.

11 WALL, Geoffrey, and WRIGHT, Cynthia, 1977, *Environmental Impact of Outdoor Recreation*, ISBN 0-921083-08-4, 69 pp.

10 RUSSWURM, Lorne H., PRESTON, Richard E., and MARTIN, Larry R.G., 1977, *Essays on Canadian Urban Process and Form*, 377 pp. (Available only in microfiche).

9   HYMA, B., and RAMESH, A., 1977, *Cholera and Malaria Incidence in Tamil, Nadu, India: Case Studies in Medical Geography*, 322 pp. (Available only in microfiche).

8   WALKER, David F., editor, 1977, *Industrial Services*, ISBN 0-921083-07-6, 107 pp.

7   BOYER, Jeanette C., 1977, *Human Response to Frost Hazards in the Orchard Industry, Okanagan Valley, British Columbia*, 207 pp. (Available only in microfiche).

6   BULLOCK, Ronald A., 1975, *Ndeiya, Kikuyu Frontier: The Kenya Land Problem in Microcosm*, ISBN 0-921083-06-8, 144 pp.

5   MITCHELL, Bruce, editor, 1975, *Institutional Arrangements for Water Management: Canadian Experiences*, 225 pp. (Available only in microfiche).

4   PATRICK, Richard A., 1975, *Political Geography and the Cyprus Conflict: 1963-1971*, 481 pp. (Available only in microfiche).

3   WALKER, David F., and BATER, James H., editors, 1974, *Industrial Development in Southern Ontario: Selected Essays*, 306 pp. (Available only in microfiche).

2   PRESTON, Richard E., editor, 1973, *Applied Geography and the Human Environment: Proceedings of the Fifth International Meeting, Commission on Applied Geography, International Geographical Union*, 397 pp. (Available only in microfiche).

1   McLELLAN, Alexander G., editor, 1971, *The Waterloo County Area: Selected Geographical Essays*, ISBN 0-921083-04-1, 316 pp.